Cooperative Research in U.S. Manufacturing

Assessing Policy Initiatives and Corporate Strategies

Albert N. Link
University of North Carolina at Greensboro

Laura L. Bauer
Quick, Finan and Associates

Lexington Books
D.C. Heath and Company/Lexington, Massachusetts/Toronto

338.4767
L75c

Library of Congress Cataloging-in-Publication Data

Link, Albert N.
    Cooperative research in U.S. manufacturing.

    Bibliography: p.
    Includes index.
    1. United States—Manufactures—Research.
2. Research, Industrial—United States. I. Bauer,
Laura L. II. Title. III. Title: Cooperative research
in US manufacturing.
HD9725.L56   1989   338.4'767'0973   87–45771
ISBN 0–669–16969–2 (alk. paper)

Published simultaneously in Canada
Printed in the United States of America
International Standard Book Number: 0–669–16969–2
Library of Congress Catalog Card Number 87–45771

The paper used in this publication meets the minimum requirements of American National
Standard for Information Sciences—Permanence of Paper for Printed Library Materials,
ANSI Z39.48–1984. ∞™

88   89   90   91   92   8   7   6   5   4   3   2   1

For our families

Contents

8. Summary Statement   99

Figures and Tables

Figures

Tables

Foreword

It is only a slight exaggeration to say that the paradigms of standard economic theory admit of two types of firm behavior—internalization and arm's-length transactions. The explanation of interfirm cooperation is, at best, beclouded by uncertainty about the proper motivational assumptions. But whatever the specific nature of these assumptions, there seems to exist less doubt about the fact that the outcome of any form of cooperation tends to be anti-competitive. Hovering in the background, of course, is the notorious history of manufacturers' cartels, whose "cooperation" resulted in the blocking of new developments, the withholding of new products, and the restriction of markets.

The conventional wisdom of economics stands in contrast to the postulates of a rapidly growing literature on business strategy, which recognizes various forms of cooperative arrangements as important competitive weapons, especially in the context of global rivalry. Under the impact of this rivalry, American legislative and regulatory attitudes toward interfirm cooperation have moved, albeit cautiously, in the direction of greater permissiveness. This trend has been most apparent with respect to the activities somewhat vaguely subsumed under the terms *research and development*. Rightly or wrongly, the underlying rationalization was that a strengthening of American industries' technological bases formed the key to their survival in world markets.

While a number of studies have documented the significant role of cooperation among foreign firms and among large, multinational enterprises, little has so far been known about the strategic responses of American companies to what is clearly a changing environment. To be sure, anecdotal evidence suggested a greater readiness to form partnerships for the purpose of exploiting complementarities and scale economies in R&D, but systematic information about the form and extent of such joint work has been lacking.

Link and Bauer deserve credit for having taken an important step toward remedying this situation. Their study is the result of an admirable effort to gather comprehensive empirical evidence, not by contemplating published statistics, but by undertaking an actual survey of a sample of companies. The findings shed light on several issues. Most significant, perhaps, is the extent to which international competitive pressures have motivated managements to undertake cooperative ventures in technology development. For once, public perceptions, formed mainly on the basis of a vast body of exhortative writings, appear to be accurate: "globalization" has indeed changed the rules of the game!

One can only wish that this book may find a wide readership. Economists will be pleased by how well Link and Bauer have managed to integrate their work into the body of received knowledge. Students of business strategy should find many of their conjectures supported by solid analysis. And, practicing managers might well regard the conclusions drawn from the survey as valuable background to their own thinking about strategic decision making.

Gerhard Rosegger

* Frank Tracy Carlton Professor of Economics, Case Western Reserve University.

Acknowledgments

As with any lengthy undertaking, many individuals contribute in one way or another to the effort. This was also the case with this book.

First, we are pleased to acknowledge the National Science Foundation, Division of Policy Research and Analysis, for its financial support of this project. In January 1985, that division solicited proposals to examine aspects of the topic "The Influence of Size of Firm, Private Contracted Research, and Industry Structure on Private R&D and Innovation." We were fortunate to be awarded a research grant to study cooperative research activity among U.S. manufacturing firms as part of that solicitation (PRA85-212664).

Second, we would like to thank all of those individual who offered suggestions on earlier versions of much of the material presented in this book, especially Professor Kathy Combs and Professor Terry Seaks. An earlier version of Chapter 4 was presented at the economics workshop at Case Western Reserve University. Also, many of the concepts posited in Chapter 5 were presented at the 1987 International Society for Product Innovation Management Meetings at Brighton Polytechnic Institute, England. The comments and suggestions from both groups were extremely useful.

As always, our colleagues at the University of North Carolina at Greensboro provided valuable assistance and exhibited much patience as the book progressed. We are especially thankful to Professor Gerhard Rosegger for writing the foreword of this book.

1
Introduction

In 1987 the editorial staff of the *Harvard Business Review* asked its readers, "Do you think there is a competitiveness problem?" The answer from nearly 4,000 respondents was overwhelmingly "yes." The results of the *Harvard Business Review* query indicate that 92 percent of the respondents think that U.S. competitiveness is deteriorating. As a result of this deterioration, they believe that their standard of living and the U.S. world economic position, are threatened.

The popular press is replete with indictments regarding where to place the burden of responsibility for this situation. The gamut of culprits includes, as one might expect, managers, the federal government, and workers. Hardly surprising, the range of solutions suggested to alleviate the competitiveness problem is equally as encompassing: more effective management, more directed government policies, and an improved work ethic on the part of labor.

It has previously been suggested that the competitive survival of U.S. corporations rests, in large part, in more defined areas. The competitive survival of U.S. corporations rests, in our opinion, on the adoption and implementation of technology-based strategies.[1] Successful technology-based strategies require a balanced integration of internal corporate organization, internal sources of technology, and strategic planning coupled with external sources of strategy-relevant information. In other words, those firms that are able to compete successfully in international markets will be those that combine internal and external components into a single, technology-based integrated strategy. According to Robert M. White, president of the National Academy of Engineering, "This country's problem is not the lack of basic research but inadequate conversion of scientific discovery to commercialization."[2]

How is such an integrated competitive strategy to be implemented? Perhaps the most common response by managers and public policy makers to such a question is that corporations should increase their research and development (R&D) activity. The implicit assumption behind such a simple prescription is that increases in R&D will enhance innovativeness and thus improve the competitive position of firms in the international community. The logic behind this prescription is that R&D spending within a firm leads to innovations within that firm, which lead to enhanced productivity and, thus, a competitive advantage in the market place. In other words,

$$R\&D \longrightarrow \text{innovation} \longrightarrow \text{productivity improvements}$$

Noteworthy is the fact that the initial policy response to the slowdown in the productivity growth of most U.S. industries in the mid-1970s was the R&D tax credit portion of the Economic Recovery and Tax Act of 1981.[3]

Historically, an R&D-focused strategy, such as that just modeled, did have merit. However, today there is a new order of competition in the world. Firms no longer have the luxury of investing in R&D and waiting for the resulting technology to develop and become embodied in their production process. Such a linear strategy is too time intensive and it will result in technologically obsolete products because the competition is moving much too quickly. Gone are the days when firms could formulate their competitive strategies on the premise that investments in scientific knowledge will, with time and patience, lead to profitable discoveries.

It is doubtful if innovative experiences like those at Du Pont, for example, will typify the technology-based strategies of competitively successful firms. Firms no longer have the luxury of investing solely in internal fundamental research that, over time, will lead to major product successes such as nylon or teflon. This is not to say that major breakthroughs will occur overnight. Rather, U.S. corporate strategies must acknowledge the fact that there are world competitors who are reaching the development stage faster than they are. Catch-up is a difficult—and often an unprofitable—position to be in.

Competition is growing at the R&D stage. Technologies are evolving, penetrating, and maturing much faster today than ever before. It is reasonable to expect that this pace will continue to increase, too. This fact comes from more rapid advances in generic technology by foreign industries based on government support and on their cooperative research activities, and from more intense *world* competition, which brings about a faster penetration and maturation of products. Simply stated, cycles are evolving at faster rates, and strategic responses must keep pace.

One response to this new order of world competition is for firms to look beyond their own R&D as the dominant source of new technical knowledge. Firms need to think in broader terms: firms need to look toward strategic alliances as a mechanism for increasing the speed at which new technology is developed.[4] Terry Loucks, vice-president for technology at Norton Company, articulates this view very well:

With the increased status of *knowledge* [as an] *asset* in business has come the need to explore new techniques for finding, assimilating, maintaining, and creating knowledge. Part of this search has brought about the many "new alliances" between industry. . . . There are those who believe that the partnership[s] involved in these "new alliances" represent the first modest but critical step for our nation on a journey back to competitive vitality in a global economy.[5]

Cooperation in research is not a new concept. In 1879, Thomas A. Edison, the founder of the General Electric Company, teamed up with Corning Glass Works to make the first incandescent light bulb.[6] There are many similar cases in industrial history.

Nils Wilhjelm, Denmark's minister of industry, presented the opening address at the European Industrial Research Management Association's 1987 conference on Cooperation in R&D. There he remarked:

Technological competitiveness is of vital importance for success on the export markets and is not only beneficial to the export possibilities of each individual country, but also essential for the creation of better life quality at all levels in society. It is well known that at the end of this Century, . . . industrial development has been an important factor in the process of removing unpleasant and inappropriate aspects of former times' industrialization. Increasingly, today's innovations are the products of teamwork rather than earlier times' individuals. The scope of this teamwork is becoming ever broader and comprises to a still higher degree cooperation between industry, universities and institutions of higher education, also across national borders. The individual company securing its continuous development by itself has now become history. To obtain results, it is today necessary to cooperate . . . between industry and centres of knowledge, nationally as well as internationally.[7]

In November 1987, *High Technology Business* reported a part of its interview with James Olson, then chairman of American Telephone and Telegraph. When asked, "What can U.S. businesses do to maintain their technological position?" he responded:

I think you're going to see more [research] cooperation between the major companies, particularly in some of the major fields, such as microelectronics. When I look at what it costs us [at AT&T] to fund basic research in semiconductor technology, my own personal theory is that you're going to see more and more cooperation between larger companies in the United States to be sure we stay on the leading edge.[8]

Public policies have been enacted in this country to encourage cooperative research ventures among firms, and the amount of cooperative research activity is perceived to be increasing. But surprisingly, very little is known about the economics of cooperative research. That is, very little is known about the types of firms that participate in these research relationships, the motives for their participation, or the results of the cooperative endeavors. This book is an initial attempt to shed some light on these vitally important topics.

In chapter 2, we define cooperative research. At first blush, this undertaking may seem trivial or even unnecessary; however, the term *cooperative research* is becoming such a commonplace phrase that some standardization of the concept is necessary.

In chapter 3, we present a brief overview of some recent public policy initiatives directed toward R&D. Although a more complete analysis can be found elsewhere,[9] our intent in presenting this overview is to set the stage for a more detailed discussion of policies directed toward cooperative research ventures.

In chapter 4, we discuss the characteristics of firms that engage in cooperative research activities. This chapter represents, to our knowledge, the first systematic, empirical effort to document and analyze cooperative research activities among U.S. corporations.

In chapter 5, we describe the various strategic motives associated with firms' involvement in cooperative research. The opening remarks of this chapter state that, if firms are to compete successfully in world markets, they will have to implement technology-based strategies that rely on generic technology coming from, among other places, research alliances with other firms.

In chapter 6, we evaluate some of the economic consequences associated with cooperative research. One fact that predicated the passage of the National Cooperative Research Act of 1984 was the belief that corporate responses to the act would increase the overall level of industrial R&D, especially in the waning manufacturing sector. We offer some preliminary evidence to that fact, as well as quantify the influence of cooperation on productivity growth and evaluate the efficiency with which internal R&D is conducted.

In chapter 7, we offer some subjective observations about various managerial issues associated with research cooperation as an organizational form. By doing this, we hope to provide some useful guideposts to those currently engaged in cooperative research efforts and to those who are or will be contemplating such alliances.

Finally, in chapter 8, we provide a summary of our analysis.

2
The Nature of Cooperative Research

The quoted remarks of AT&T Chairman James Olson in the introductory chapter may have created some dissonance. *Cooperation* and *competition* are not generally viewed as complementary concepts. An economist cannot help but to recall the wisdom of Adam Smith on a similar theme:[1]

> People of the same trade seldom meet together, even for merriment and diversion, but the conversation ends in a conspiracy against the public, or in some contrivance to raise prices. It is impossible indeed to prevent such meetings, by any law which either could be executed, or would be consistent with liberty and justice. But though the law cannot hinder people of the same trade from sometimes assembling together, it ought to do nothing to facilitate such assemblies, much less to render them necessary.

It is unlikely to be the case that cooperative research activities will lead to a "conspiracy" against the state, although there is a history of antitrust concerns regarding cooperation in research, as we shall discuss in the next chapter. It is important to note that cooperation at any stage of production brings a new perspective to the notion of competition.

A Definition of Cooperative Research

We use the term *cooperative research* to refer to *an arrangement through which firms jointly acquire technical knowledge*. Such arrangements can exist with partners from a number of sectors within the economy or even from overseas. Our interest here is with private sector cooperative relationships, although industry-university relationships are certainly an important research marriage to consider. Industry-government research relationships are also important but are beyond the scope of this study.

It could be argued that our definition of cooperative research is overly broad to have much meaning for corporate or even policy decision making. Our definition does not distinguish between formal and informal cooperative agreements among participating firms. Although such a distinction is valid, it is our impression from extensive interviews with R&D vice presidents (discussed in later chapters) that cooperative research–active firms make little distinction between informal relationships and formal relationships, such as a research joint venture or a research consortium arrangement, when formulating their strategic objectives.

A research joint venture (RJV), has been defined (perhaps too restrictively) as the formation of a new organization (a child) jointly controlled by at least two parent corporations for the purpose of conducting R&D.[2] Although there was some reluctance among firms to engage in this organizational research form in prior years owing to antitrust uncertainties, per se joint ventures among high technology firms have occurred for decades. Kathryn Harrigan provides an excellent history of such high technology joint ventures.[3]

A closely aligned concept is that of the research consortium. A research consortium generally exists when there is a significant public good component to the research agenda.[4] Equity shares in consortia may or may not be issued. Often, firms in high technology industries jointly fund basic research in the consortium's laboratory. Frequently, as in the case of Microelectronics and Computer Technology Corporation (MCC), founded in 1983 to engage in advanced long-term R&D directed toward various aspects of microelectronic technology such as computer aided design, a consortium's research facilities are tied to a university (the University of Texas in this case). Other well-known consortia are the Semiconductor Research Corporation (SRC), founded in 1982 to conduct research supportive of the semiconductor industry, and the Battelle Optoelectronics Research Program, formed in 1985 for research in optoelectronics, particularly the manufacturing aspects of that technology.

We view RJVs and consortia arrangements as formal cooperative research relationships. Whereas these research forms have indeed attracted the lion's share of attention in public policy circles, in the popular press, and in the academic literature, we show in Chapter 4 that the majority of cooperative research activities undertaken by corporations in the U.S. manufacturing sector are informal in their organizational design, thus justifying a broader definition.

Cooperative Research and the Process of Technology Development

Cooperative research is a mechanism through which firms in an industry can enrich the generic technology base upon which it relies in the develop-

inputs ⟶ production ⟶ economic value

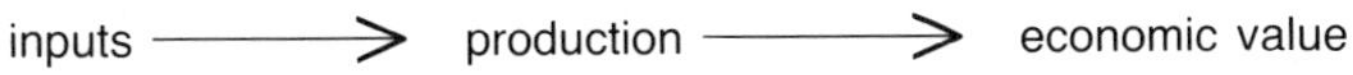

Figure 2–1. A Simple Model of Economic Activity

ment of new technology.[5] They accomplish this by investing in research that produces generic technical knowledge. Cooperative research is not the only means by which firms can invest in generic technology; however, it is lower in cost than other methods, owing to the sharing of R&D expenses. It also results in the creation of generic technology at a faster rate than if a firm undertook the related investigations as a part of its internal R&D program. To illustrate the role of cooperative research as a facilitator of generic technology, it is important first to understand the elements related to the process of technology development and to distinguish among the roles performed by internal R&D and R&D undertaken cooperatively.

Consider the model of economic activity shown in figure 2–1. This model illustrates the simple notion that inputs, through production, are transformed into output (goods or services), which takes on economic value in the marketplace.

It is common in economics to think of four input groups that combine to produce output (Q). These groups include labor inputs (L), capital inputs (K), material inputs (M), and technology inputs (T). It is sufficient for this discussion to think of the production process that combines inputs into output as a "black box," as shown in figure 2–2. Economists often model this transformation process by writing a production function algebraically as

$$Q = f(L, K, M, T)$$

Our particular focus is on the technology input. Specifically, we are interested in the various sources of technical knowledge that, when combined, produce the technology input.

Technology can enter a firm in many forms. Proprietary technology comes as a result of the self-financed R&D efforts of a firm. Purchased technology is, as the name suggests, developed by others and purchased by the firm. This so-called purchased technology usually takes the form of a licensing arrangement, but it conceivably could enter the firm through a

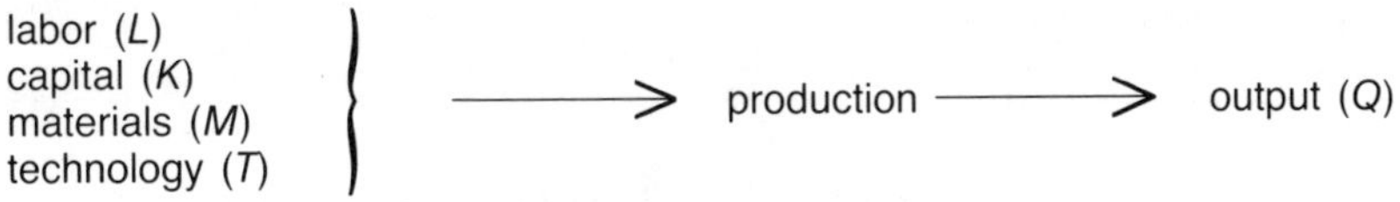

labor (L)
capital (K)
materials (M)
technology (T)
⟶ production ⟶ output (Q)

Figure 2–2. A Model of the Production Process

merger. Proprietary technology and purchased technology are illustrated, along with the concepts from figures 2–1 and 2–2, in figure 2–3.

As stated in Chapter 1, we believe that firms must think in terms of a technology-based strategy that is broader than that implied in Figure 2–3. This strategy must go beyond internal R&D budgeting. Sole reliance on their own R&D to develop proprietary technology or on licensing other's technology will not improve the competitive position of firms in the international community. Supporting, or leveraging, the efficiency with which proprietary and purchased technology are used in the production process are two other technological elements: generic technology and infratechnology.

Generic technology and the associated research process represent the organization of knowledge into the conceptual form of an eventual application and the laboratory testing of the concept. The foundation for generic technology is the science base, which comes from and is enhanced by basic research funded primarily by the public sector. But, unlike the fundamental scientific principles that constitute the science base, generic technology has a functional focus. For example, the basic design concepts and architecture of integrated circuits are a generic technology.

Infratechnologies are a less widely recognized technological element. As the name implies, infratechnologies support the technological base of all firms in an industry. As such, they have a neutral competitive influence. Infratechnologies include evaluated scientific data used in the conduct of R&D; measurement and test methods used in research, production control, and acceptance testing for market transactions; and various technical procedures such as those used in the calibration of equipment. Infratechnologies facilitate development of the generic technology, as well as the proprietary and purchased technology, by, for example, providing highly precise measurements and creating organized and evaluated scientific and engineering data necessary for understanding, characterizing, and interpreting relevant research findings.

Figure 2–4 builds upon figure 2–3 to present a more complete model

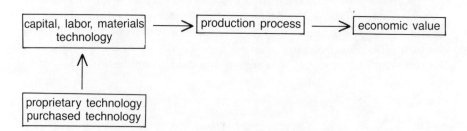

Figure 2–3. A Myopic Model of Technological Development

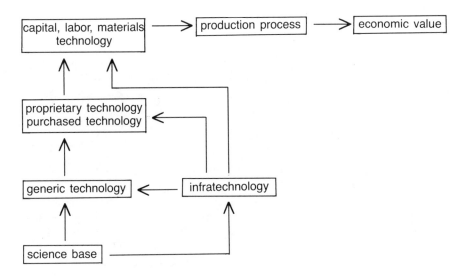

Figure 2–4. A Complete Model of Technological Development

of technological development. Generic technology is shown to relate directly to the way in which a firm's own R&D augments the production process. Cooperative research endeavors are generally aimed at generic technology research. By enriching the generic technology base, internal R&D is performed more efficiently, and the speed at which the process of technology development occurs increases, too. These ideas about the role of cooperative research can be illustrated in an alternative way by introducing two related constructs: the product life cycle and the production process life cycle.

The product life cycle is well known to both students and practitioners of management. Although many varieties of this concept exist, the basic idea represented by the product life cycle is that sales of a product in an industry increase and then, as the product matures and as competing products enter the market, sales decrease. This idea is illustrated in figure 2–5. Total industry sales are considered on the vertical axis and time is considered on the horizontal axis. Four stages are noted on this figure. Industry sales increase very slowly beginning at time period t^* as the new product is first introduced. Sales then increase rapidly during the growth stage (assuming that the market accepts the product). As the market nears saturation, the growth in sales begins to decline during the maturity stage. Finally, in the decline stage, sales fall. Presumably, as this particular product enters the maturity stage, some other competing product is beginning its introduction stage. The length of time associated with the cycle as a whole, or with any one stage within the cycle, is specific to the product in question.

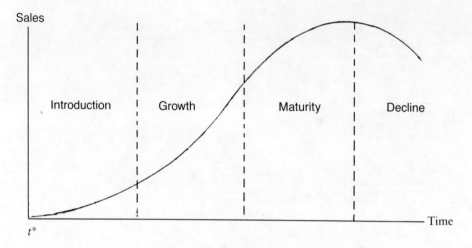

Figure 2–5. The Product Life Cycle

Prior to time t^*, innovative activity was occurring in which the underlying technology was being developed and first applied.[6] This premarket activity occurs in what many call an *entrepreneurial stage*. If the adjective *entrepreneurial* refers only to inventiveness, then such a characterization has some meaning. But, we offer a word of caution about the concept of entrepreneurship used in that way. A careful reading of the historical literature on the concept of the entrepreneur—who an entrepreneur is and what an entrepreneur does—refers to an entrepreneur as one who takes risk and as one who perceives opportunities.[7] In this context, every stage in the life cycle is an entrepreneurial stage, although perceptions of risk may vary with time. Managers throughout the industry exhibit entrepreneurlike talent every day.

The production process life cycle is a closely aligned concept,[8] with three stages of a technology's evolution: a fluid stage, a transitional stage, and a specific stage. In the fluid stage, the product technology and the process producing the technology are very general, undergoing frequent changes. Production is relatively labor-intensive and the capital in place is of a general-purpose nature so as to accommodate changes in form and design. Accordingly, products are undergoing frequent design changes as the market begins to evolve toward a standard, or dominant, design. Also, there is a great deal of product diversity among producers in the industry.

Process developments in production become more important in the transitional stage in response to competition based on increased output volume and cost. This stage is characterized by increased entry and product standardization plus a realization of scale economies. Capital thus becomes more specialized in response to the dominant product design and related industrial standards.

During the specific stage, in response to the emergence of a dominant product standard, firms compete—through more advanced process technologies—on the basis of cost, quality, reliability, and so forth. These technologies develop in the supplying markets in response to the standardized product design. The three stages of development are frequently used to illustrate the fact that once a new product is introduced, product innovation declines in favor of cost-reducing process innovation (see table 2–1). Here, we superimpose these three stages of development onto the product life cycle in order to illustrate the rate of internal R&D spending over time.

The diagram in figure 2–5 is reproduced in the top portion of figure 2–6. The lower diagram in figure 2–6 illustrates the pattern of internal R&D spending that parallels the life cycle for a representative firm. R&D spending in the fluid stage follows a base-line pattern, primarily aimed at product development, and it supports the evolution of the emerging dominant product design. During the transitional stage, R&D spending increases. Product R&D increases to help the firm capture the greatest market share, and process R&D increases in an effort to reduce production costs (which begin to rise rapidly during the growth stage of the product life cycle). Some process R&D is allocated toward internal cost reduction whereas another portion is allocated toward modifying suppliers' capital equipment in an effort to meet the firm's specific requirement set. R&D spending tapers off in the transitional stage.

We stated previously that cooperative research is a means through which firms in a technology-active industry can enrich the generic technology base upon which they rely in the development of new technology. We also suggested that such research alliances will be necessary if firms are to compete successfully in world markets in the years ahead. As a result of the rapid advances in generic technology by foreign firms, owing to the increased government support and cooperative research efforts in selected industries within these countries and owing to the scale phenomenon that

Table 2–1.
Key Aspects of the Production Process Life Cycle

Stage of Development	Relevant Characteristics
Fluid	Rapid, frequent product changes; product diversity
Transitional	Emergence of a dominant product design; maturing product group; process specialization
Specific	Emergence of a dominant process design; intergrated automated process technology; reliance on suppliers' technology

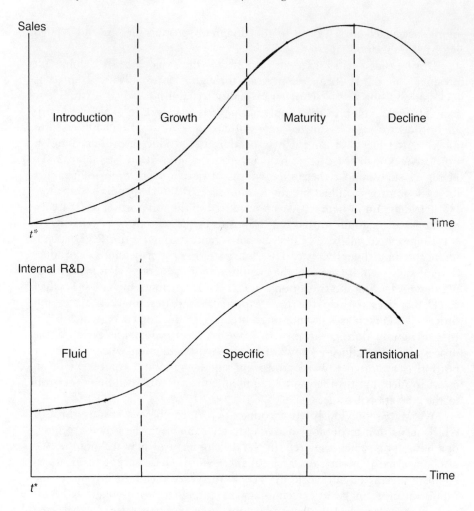

Figure 2–6. Technological Developments and the Product Life Cycle

there are more technologically-capable participants in world markets today, products are being introduced into the marketplace and they are penetrating the market at a faster rate than in the past. Through cooperation, U.S. firms can truncate the entire R&D-dependent cycles shown in figure 2–6. That is, through cooperative research, U.S. firms will be able to meet the pace at which new, technology-based products are entering the market. By so doing, the product life cycle compresses and shifts to the left, that is, the speed of introduction increases. Similarly, cooperative research in generic technology will increase the efficiency with which internal R&D is conducted, thus reducing the R&D cost per product technology and thereby diverting more internal funding to future generations of technology.

Strategic Reliance on Cooperative Research

A "cooperative" research endeavor between the Industrial Technology Program at the University of North Carolina at Greensboro and the Technology Information and Policy Program at Syracuse University began in 1982. In that year, 146 R&D-active U.S. manufacturing firms from the *Fortune* 1000 were surveyed as part of a pilot study to document the use of alternative sources of technology used by such firms.[9]

Two subsequent questionnaires were administered to this group of firms in an effort to quantify their use of alternative mechanisms for acquiring and developing new technologies. These surveys were administered in late 1982 and again in 1985. There were 117 respondents (out of 146) in 1982 and 102 (out of 146) in 1985. In both years, the sample of responding firms accounted for just over 30 percent of the total company-financed R&D conducted in the manufacturing sector.

In each of these two years, the firms were asked to respond to the following question, "How important are each of the following sources for new technology in your corporation's overall technology-based competitive strategy?" The four general source categories were internal R&D programs, licensing of others' technology, mergers to acquire another firm's technology, and cooperative research ventures. Each firm's R&D vice-president was asked to respond to this question using a five-point Likert scale ranging from "very important" (= 5) to "not important at all" (= 1). The mean responses to this question are reported in table 2–2.

Several patterns are immediately evident from the mean responses presented in this table. First, the R&D vice-presidents of the responding firms view their own R&D efforts as the most fundamental element of their firm's technology-based competitive strategy. This is not surprising on two

Table 2–2.
Mean Rank of Alternative Sources of Technology

Source	1982 Response (n = 117)	1985 Response (n = 102)
Internal R&D	4.2	4.1
Licensing	1.7	1.9
Mergers	3.1	2.2
Cooperative Research	2.5	3.7

Key: 5 = very important; 1 = not important at all.

counts: one, the survey was administered to the most senior R&D officer in each corporation; and two, the firms in the sample are large and have a long history of R&D activity.

Second, there appears in the data to have been a decrease in merger activity as a mechanism through which firms acquire new technology. This finding is not at odds with the general decline in merger activity that characterized the manufacturing sector as a whole in the early to mid-1980s (but this trend is not reversing itself).

Third, the data also reveal that there has been an increase in the use of cooperative research for acquiring new technology. Although the firms in this sample were not queried as to the strategic motivation for their involvement in cooperative research, the 1982–1985 period is one in which technology-based foreign competition increased and the health of the American economy was strong.

Finally, the increase in the relative importance of cooperative research, as compared to mergers, is perhaps indicative of the realization that cooperating partners gain a competitive edge from such ventures. Generic technology has many of the characteristics of a public good, and thus the results from the cooperative endeavors are generally firm-neutral. All firms are better off as a result of a successful cooperation.

The result of the data just presented is that clearly R&D vice-presidents perceive that cooperative research activities are an important external source of technology development. This data set does not permit a sophisticated examination of the reasons why the relative importance of cooperation increased over this time period. Perhaps the time was just right for an alternative competitive strategy. According to Bobby R. Inman, former chairman of MCC, when commenting on the formation of his research consortia: "Without the spur of the Japanese competition in the marketplace, these [microelectronics] companies would never have agreed to work together."[10] Or, as we discuss in the following chapter, perhaps the competitive climate in this country changed at an appropriate time. According to William C. Norris, chairman and chief executive officer of Control Data Corporation and MCC's conceptualizer: "Fundamentally, companies didn't want to cooperate, and they found antitrust laws a really good reason not to . . . but it wasn't until a lot of these companies had the hell scared out of them by the Japanese that they were willing to give it a try."[11] More specifically,

> Traditionally, U.S. companies have largely shunned technological cooperation. The primary reasons have been their failure to perceive the benefits, the unwillingness by executives to share decision making, undue concern for proprietary position, and fears of antitrust action. In this period of scarce resources, however, and at a time when this country's leading posi-

tion in technology is being challenged by foreign competitors, refusal to cooperate is no longer tenable. . . . The stage is set for industry initiatives to expand R&D cooperation rapidly.[12]

Concluding Statement

The descriptive data presented in this chapter raise many more questions about the nature of cooperative research than they answer. After a brief historical overview of public policies related to cooperation in the next chapter, we turn in Chapters 4, 5, and 6 to a more detailed empirical analysis of the nature of cooperative research among firms in the U.S. manufacturing sector.

3
Public Policy and Cooperative Research

The economic rationale for public support of industrial R&D, in general, is based on the theoretical criterion guiding the allocation of goods and services between the public and private sectors. Government intervention is said to be justified whenever there is a market failure. Market failure can arise for a number of reasons. In the case of industrial R&D (basic and generic research, in particular), market failure is a result of features intrinsic to the nature of information per se. Innovation involves the process of creating information, and information has characteristics of a public good.

Public Policy Directed toward R&D

Public policies directed toward innovation have long been directed specifically toward R&D spending. Support for industrial research programs can be traced as far back as the 1780s with the U.S. Navy's sponsored research programs. Since World War II, direct federal support of R&D has been tied to military- and defense-related research. In 1954, Section 174 of the Internal Revenue Code was adopted, which codified and expanded tax laws pertaining to firms' R&D expenditures. Businesses were allowed to deduct the costs of research and experimentation in the year in which they were incurred. Many view this legislation as the first formal tax incentive directed toward R&D.[1]

Several important incentives for increasing R&D investments came from the Reagan administration's policy centerpiece, the Economic Recovery Tax Act of 1981. Most notable is the singling out of R&D for special treatment, based on the presumption that investments in R&D are closely tied to technological change and that technological change leads to productivity growth. Productivity growth in the U.S. private economy had been decreasing since the mid-1960s, with an accelerated decline beginning in the early 1970s.[2]

This tax act permitted, for the first time, industrial firms to receive a tax credit equalling 25 percent of the amount by which their qualified research expenses during a given year exceeded the base level of such expenses. The base-period level was defined as the average qualified expenses of the three previous years. Qualified research expenses are those defined in keeping with Section 174 of the Internal Revenue Code. If a firm pays other parties to conduct the R&D, only 65 percent of those payments qualify as research expenditures for tax credit purposes.

Analyses of the effectiveness of this tax credit as a mechanism to increase R&D expenditures, and thereby to spur productivity growth, suggest that the impact of the tax credit is, thus far, less than anticipated.[3] One explanation is that firms committed to a long-run, technology-based competitive strategy are unlikely to be affected by marginal incentives. As stated by Richard Mahoney of Monsanto Corporation, a significant tax change would not alter his company's investment plans: "We don't operate on the margin" implying that tax changes make little difference to the strategic direction of his corporation.[4]

We do not argue that tax policies toward R&D are unimportant per se. Tax policy is only one of several macroeconomic factors that affect corporate decision making along with inflation and interest rate changes. It is important to recall one relevant aspect of the process of technological development shown in figure 2–4 and in table 2–2. Firms rely not only on internal R&D as a source of technology, but they also rely on purchased technologies (part of which may be embodied in new capital) and on cooperative research. Thus, at best, an R&D tax credit will affect a given firm's technology base directly in only one dimension (unless it is assumed that the R&D tax credit affects the firm in question through increased innovativeness on the part of those conducting the research that is ultimately purchased—over time, this may or may not be the case).

National Cooperative Research Act of 1984

An important result of the White House Domestic Policy Review of Industrial Innovation in 1978 and 1979 was President Carter's charge to the Department of Justice to clarify its position on collaboration between firms in the area of research. It was his belief that antitrust laws should not be "mistakenly understood to prevent cooperative activity, even in circumstances where it would foster innovation without harming competition."[5]

In response, in November 1980, the Department of Justice issued its *Antitrust Guide Concerning Research Joint Ventures* that includes several important premises upon which the legislation leading to the passage of the National Cooperative Research Act of 1984 are implicitly based. The *Guide* states that

Research itself presents a broad spectrum of activity, from "pure" basic research into fundamental principles, on the one hand, to development research focusing on promotional differentiation of a product or marketing issues on the other extreme. In general, basic research is undertaken with less predictability of outcome, and thus more risk, than developmental research. Moreover, *the outcomes of basic research are less likely to be appropriable and thus more likely to be widely diffused in the economy, with the possibility of there being the basis of future advance and competitive opportunity for all.* [emphasis added]

The intensity of antitrust concerns about joint research will vary along the research spectrum: less intense about "pure" basic research, undertaken without ancillary restraints on use of the results, to more intense at the developmental end of the research spectrum, particularly if ancillary restraints are involved. A pure research joint venture without ancillary restraints has never been challenged by the Antitrust Division. . . . Nevertheless . . . concern has been expressed that valuable joint research efforts, particularly in basic research, might be deterred by fear, possibly unwarranted, of exposure to antitrust attack.

In general, the closer the joint activity is to the basic end of the research spectrum—i.e., the further removed it is from substantial market effects and developmental issues—the more likely it is to be acceptable under the antitrust laws.[6]

Several bills concerned explicitly with R&D joint ventures were introduced in the 98th session of Congress. The Thurmond Bill would have excused all R&D joint ventures from existing provisions of antitrust law related to the award of treble damages in successful suits. The Glenn and the Rodino Bill were aimed at relaxing all antitrust regulations serving as barriers to R&D joint ventures. The Mathias Bill was even more comprehensive and included measures for sharing patent and royalty rights coming from cooperative ventures. Much of the thought behind these bills crystallized into the Joint Research and Development Act of 1984 (HR 5041), and eventually was finalized as the National Cooperative Research Act of 1984 (Public Law 98-462).

The National Cooperative Research Act defines a "joint research and development venture" as

any group of activities, including attempting to make, making, or performing a contract, by two or more persons for the purpose of—

(A) theoretical analysis, experimentation, or systematic study of phenomena or observable facts,

(B) the development or testing of basic engineering techniques,

(C) the extension of investigative findings or theory of a scientific or technical nature into practical application for experimental and demonstration purposes. . .,

(D) the collection, exchange, and analysis of research information, or

(E) any combination of the [above].

The National Cooperative Research Act is explicit to exclude from this definition any exchange of information "relating to costs, sales, profitability, prices, marketing, or distribution of any product, process, or service that is not reasonably required to conduct the research and development that is the purpose of such venture." And, this act clearly prohibits agreements

> (A) to restrict or require the sale, licensing, or sharing of inventions or developments not developed through such venture, or
> (B) to restrict or require participation by such party in other research and development activities.

Clearly, this definition of a *joint research and development venture*, an RJV, is broader than pure basic research, as discussed earlier in the Department of Justice guidelines. Still, it is clear from the language of the law that the perceived output from an RJV is expected to be *information* per se.

Gene Grossman and Carl Shapiro note in their detailed analysis of RJVs that information is knowledge and that knowledge has characteristics of a public good:

> knowledge once produced has the attributes of a *public good*; the use of information by one party does not exclude simultaneous use by others at no further cost. This implies that *ex post* (that is, after discovery) economic efficiency is best served by widespread diffusion of the information. . . . An RJV . . . will automatically ensure the diffusion of the products of the research effort to at least the subset of firms that participate in the venture.[7]

The two primary objectives of the National Cooperative Research Act are to establish a rule of reason for evaluating the antitrust implications of each RJV on an individual case basis and to limit potential liability to actual damages rather than treble damages (as is more common under antitrust law). According to the act,

> In any action under the antitrust laws, or under any State law similar to the antitrust laws, the conduct of any person in making and performing a contract to carry out a joint research and development venture shall not be deemed illegal per se; such conduct shall be judged on the basis of its *reasonableness* [emphasis added], taking into account all relevant factors affecting competition.

And, "Notwithstanding section 4 of the Clayton Act . . . any person who is entitled to recovery on a claim . . . shall recover the actual damages sustained by such person."

In addition, the National Cooperative Research Act requires a public disclosure of joint research and development ventures. Parties in RJVs are required to file notification within 90 days with the Attorney General of the United States and with the Federal Trade Commission. This notification must disclose the identities of the parties to such ventures, as well as the nature of the venture itself. Notifications are made public, with a short lag time, in the *Federal Register*.[8]

Federal Register Filings

The National Cooperative Research Act and subsequent *Federal Register* filings relate to formal cooperative research relationships, using our terminology. As stated earlier, most of the research cooperation that takes place in the manufacturing sector is on an informal basis, and it is unlikely to be documented from perusing *Federal Register* filings; however, the information contained in these public filings is, to date, the *only* public data set related to such activity. As such, a detailed analysis of the filings is warranted as a first step toward understanding the nature of cooperative research.

Kathryn Combs has provided an initial look at a sample of the filings. From her analysis of twenty-seven of the early filings she concluded that firms in at least a few industries expect their RJV to be worthwhile, although they have devoted, on average, less than 1 percent of their total R&D budget to the endeavor. Also, it was evident from these twenty-seven filings that in no case did an entire industry participate in the research agenda.[9]

Our analysis is more encompassing; however, we reach a conclusion similar to that of Combs, namely that the information contained in the *Federal Register* filings is insufficient to allow any substantial generalizations about the nature of cooperative research activity in U.S. industry. One conclusion that can be drawn is that the types of activities reported in the filings do not conform well to any single standard definition of an RJV. What seems apparent in the *Federal Register* filings is "over filing" due to an uncertainty as to how the term *joint research and development venture* will be interpreted in antitrust practices. The act of filing may be viewed by many corporations as a low-cost way of ensuring against uncertainty. We prefer to refer to the activities reported in the *Federal Register* as formal, as opposed to informal, cooperative research ventures (CRVs).

As of December 31, 1987, seventy-seven CRVs had been filed and had been reported in the *Federal Register*. As a first step toward a more systematic analysis of the CRVs, we devised seven categories in which all of the reported CRVs could be classified.[10] These categories are

Category 1. Industry consortia conducting long-term R&D.
Category 2. Project-specific industry joint ventures.
Category 3. Research corporations with their own research facilities.
Category 4. Trade associations/research foundations.
Category 5. Research conducted to meet EPA regulations.
Category 6. University-based research centers.
Category 7. Company-funded independent research institutes.

In tables 3–1 through 3–7 we classified all of the seventy-seven CRVs into these seven categories. It should be noted that our taxonomy differs from the terminology used by others, as noted in Chapter 2.

The first two categories involve some type of industrywide cooperative research venture in which the participants, in most cases, are from the same broadly-defined industry group. Category 1, industry consortia conducting long-term R&D, includes participants whose research activities are directed toward increasing the efficiency and productivity of the industry as a whole (see table 3–1). For example, the Semiconductor Research Corporation is one nonprofit industry organization (noted in the previous chapter) organized to plan, promote, sponsor, and conduct research supportive of the semiconductor industry. Since their research mission focuses on the entire industry, it is unlikely that any one participant in this venture will gain a significant competitive advantage as a result of participation. The industry, as a whole, will be more competitive in world markets.

By contrast, the results associated with the activities of the CRVs in Category 2, project-specific industry joint ventures, are somewhat more appropriable to the participants engaged in the venture because the research is more applied in nature, compared with that associated with Category 1. For example, Intel Corporation and Xicor Corporation are engaged in cooperative activities for the joint development of EEPROM devices for manufacture (see table 3–2). Even though the technology underlying these

Table 3–1
Category 1. Industry Consortia Conducting Long-Term R&D

Filings	Date
Software Productivity Consortium	1/17/85
Computer Aided Manufacturing, International	1/24/85
Bell Communications Research, Inc. (Bellcore)	1/30/85
Semiconductor Research Corporation	1/30/85
Merrell Dow Pharmaceuticals & Hoffman-LaRoche	2/19/85
Norton/TRW Ceramics	1/28/86
International Magnesium Development Corporation	6/30/86
National Center for Manufacturing Sciences	3/17/87

Table 3–2
Category 2. Project-Specific Industry Joint Ventures

Filings	Date
Exxon Production Research and Halliburton	1/17/85
Bethlehem Steel and U.S. Steel	1/30/85
Medium Range Transmission Project	2/4/85
Uninet R&D Co.	3/1/85
Bellcore and Honeywell	3/25/85
International Partners in Glass Research	4/10/85
Oncogen	4/30/85
Kaiser and Reynolds	5/13/85
Bellcore and Racal Data	6/20/85
Bellcore and Avantek	6/28/85
Bellcore and U.S. Department of Army	6/28/85
Bellcore and HHI	8/6/85
Bellcore and ADC	9/5/85
Pump Research and Development	11/15/85
Bellcore and Hitachi	12/12/85
Intel and Xicor	12/12/85
Subsea Production Maintenance	1/4/86
Kean and Fabristeel	1/28/86
Petroleum Environmental Research Forum	3/14/86
Casting of Steel Sheet Project	6/12/86
Wickes and Cycles Peugeot	7/15/86
ARCO and Air Products	8/28/86
Babcock and Wilcox	12/24/86
Bellcore and Fujitsu	2/13/87
Bellcore et al.	2/13/87
Petroleum Environmental Research Forum (86-05)	3/25/87
Petroleum Environmental Research Forum (86-06)	3/25/87
Petroleum Environmental Research Forum (86-09)	3/25/87
Metal Casting Technology	4/1/87
Bellcore et al.	4/30/87
CPW Technology	6/15/87
Pacific Bell and Integrated Network Corp.	7/1/87
Bellcore and MSC	7/13/87
Corning and Nippon	7/15/87
Bellcore et al.	10/2/87
Corporation for Open Systems International and the National Computing Center, Ltd.	10/7/87
Corporation for Open Systems International and the National Computing Center, Ltd.	12/4/87
Bellcore and NEC	12/18/87

Table 3–3
Category 3. Research Corporations with Their Own Facilities

Filings	Date
Microelectronics and Computer Technology Corporation	1/17/85
Empire State Electric Energy Research Corp.	2/8/85
Adirondack Lakes Survey Corporation	2/8/85
International Fuel Cell Corporation	4/5/85
The Plastics Recycling Foundation	5/21/85
Applied Information Technologies Group	10/9/85
Keramont Research Corporation	4/3/86
Corporation for Open Systems International	6/11/86

devices is generic, as we defined that technological element in Chapter 2, these firms will gain a competitive advantage over other late-entrants into this specific submarket.

Category 3, research corporations with their own research facilities, is a rather distinct grouping. The participants, shown in table 3–3, are incorporated and issue equity shares to the member firms. Microelectronics and Computer Technology Corporation, for example, is in this category. MCC had twenty shareholders at the time of the initial filing. It is engaged in long-term R&D directed toward several areas of microelectronics and computer technology, such as the development of advanced computer architecture.[11]

Category 4, trade associations and research foundations, includes six organizations pursuing both technical and nontechnical activities (see table 3–4). The activities are basic in design and are intended to be firm-neutral in their application.

Category 5, research conducted to meet EPA regulations, includes, as the name suggests, organizations engaged in research to meet EPA regula-

Table 3–4
Category 4. Trade Associations and Research Foundations

Filings	Date
Center for Advanced Television Studies	2/1/85
Portland Cement Association	2/5/85
Geothermal Drilling Organization	10/29/85
NAHB Research Foundation (Smart House Project)	1/28/86
Material Handling Research Center	9/11/87
American Institute of Timber Construction et al.	10/30/87

Table 3–5
Category 5. Research Conducted to Meet EPA Regulations

Filings	Date
Motor Vehicle Manufacturing Association et al.	2/8/85
Deet Joint Research Venture	10/22/85
Pyrethrin Joint Research Venture	3/18/86
Engine Manufacturers Association et al.	7/17/86
ABDAC QUAT Joint Venture	10/7/86
Pine Oil Joint Research Venture	2/5/87
American Honda Motor Co. et al.	10/14/87

tions. The participants listed in table 3–5, in general, are not concerned with gaining a competitive advantage or improving productivity. Rather, the research is standard-specific, aimed at conducting toxicological research on pesticide ingredients, for example.

Category 6, university-based research centers, tends to include goal-oriented activities and participants (see table 3–6). Often, these centers were established with seed money from a private-sector organization or foundation for phased-in industry support. Although the basic knowledge generated from the ventures in this category is internalized by the university researcher and disseminated through publication and other academic outlets, it may be the case that many of the applied results will be appropriated by the funding corporations.

According to Herbert Fusfeld and Carmela Haklisch, the types of activities that we include in Category 7, company-funded independent research institutes, are, generally, nonproprietary in nature.[12] However, upon a close examination of the six CRVs placed under this rubric in table 3–7, and from our discussions with the various R&D managers, the participants expect that the results from these research endeavors will give them a definite competitive advantage in the future. For example, the Battelle Me-

Table 3–6
Category 6. University-Based Research Centers

Filings	Date
Agrigenetics Research Association, Ltd.	2/8/85
West Virginia University–Industry Cooperative Research Center	12/17/85
Industry University Center for Glass Research	9/10/86
Industry-University Cooperative Research Center for Software Engineering	2/9/87

Table 3–7
Category 7. Company-Funded Independent Research Institutes

Filings	Date
Optoelectronics Group Project	11/29/85
Southwest Research Institute (Trap Regeneration Project)	2/18/86
Southwest Research Institute (Rim Cracking Project)	6/11/86
Southwest Research Institute	8/26/87
Southwest Research Institute	9/18/87
Berkeley Sensor and Actuator Center	12/15/87

morial Institute is undertaking a research project for several firms in the field of optoelectronics, the Optoelectronics Group Project. Discussions with representatives from one of the funding firms revealed that they, and likely each participant, viewed this research as a direct substitute for long-term internal R&D.

These being the only data related to cooperative research activities in the public domain, an analysis of the information contained in the *Federal Register* is warranted. Nearly 60 percent of the filings, forty-six in total, are organized under an industrywide umbrella of one type or another. Of these forty-six filings, eight are in Category 1 (industry consortia conducting long-term R&D) and thirty-eight are in Category 2 (project-specific industry joint ventures). There is also considerable cross-category variation in the mean number of participants per filing. As shown in table 3–8, the mean number of participants per filing varies from a low of 3.4 in Category 2 to a high of 28.6 in Category 1. The overall mean for all seventy-seven filings is 10.3.

Most of the participants engaged in these reported research endeavors are active in R&D. For illustrative purposes we define an R&D-active firm

Table 3–8
Rank of Mean Number of Participants per Filing

Category	Mean Number	Relative Rank
1	28.6	7
2	3.4	1
3	13.6	5
4	25.5	6
5	12.7	4
6	6.5	2
7	9.2	3

Note: A relative rank of 7 represents the highest mean number.

Table 3–9
Relative Rank of the Percentage of Participants Being R&D-Active

Category	Percentage	Relative Rank
1	34.5	4
2	33.6	3
3	54.1	6
4	28.1	2
5	27.0	1
6	73.1	7
7	49.1	5

Note: A relative rank of 7 represents the highest percentage.

as one that is listed in *Business Week's* 1986 R&D Scoreboard. Using this definition, the percentage of R&D-active firms listed in the filings are reported in table 3–9, by category. Clearly, Category 6 (university-based research centers) is dominated by R&D-active firms.

In addition to this objective information, we subjectively evaluated the degree of appropriability of the information resulting from each project to the participating firms, for each of the seven categories. Appropriability decreases as the scope of the cooperative activities becomes more general in nature. The assignment of a relative rank of appropriability to each category in table 3–10 is not an axiomatic task. Our relative ranks are based not only on information contained in the filings but also on selected discussions with R&D managers in representative firms from each of the seven groups. For example, Category 1 (industry consortia conducting long-term R&D) contains firms concerned with improving productivity and efficiency within an entire industry. Obviously, it would be difficult for a participat-

Table 3–10
Rank of the Degree of Appropriability of Research Results

Category	Relative Rank
1	1
2	7
3	4
4	2
5	3
6	5
7	6

Note: A relative rank of 7 represents the highest degree of appropriability.

ing firm to appropriate significantly more of the related knowledge than a nonparticipating firm.

The general information in tables 3–8 through 3–10 is used to test two hypotheses. First, do the categories characterized by the greatest degree of appropriability (table 3–10) have the fewest average number of participants per filing (table 3–8)? A priori, one would think that the potential for appropriability is related to the extent to which potential users are excluded from obtaining immediate access to the research information. Thus, it follows that the degree of appropriability and the average number of participants per filing should be inversely related. As shown in table 3–11, the Spearman rank order correlation coefficient is -0.93, indicating that such an inverse relationship exists and it is significant.

Second, do the categories characterized by the greatest degree of appropriability have the greatest percentage of R&D-active members (table 3–9)? A priori, one would think that the potential for obtaining research results that yield a competitive advantage is related to experience in research endeavors per se. Thus, it follows that the degree of appropriability and the percentage of categorical participants that are R&D-active should be positively related. As shown in table 3–12, the Spearman rank order correlation is indeed positive, 0.32, but it is not significant at a conventional level. As an explanation, it is possible that research experience might be more properly quantified in terms of a variable that reflects *scope* as well as *scale*. This endeavor is beyond the capacity of the data.

Table 3–11
Rank Order Correlation between the Mean Number of Participants per Filing and the Degree of Appropriability

Category	Relative Rank of Categories by Degree of Appropriability (7 = highest degree of appropriability)	Relative Rank of Categories by Mean Number of Participants (7 = highest mean number of participants)
1	1	7
2	7	1
3	4	5
4	2	6
5	3	4
6	5	2
7	6	3

Note: Spearman r_s = -0.93. Correlation coefficient is significant at the .01 level.

Table 3–12
Rank Order Correlation between the Percentage of R&D-Active
Participants and the Degree of Appropriability

Category	Relative Rank of Categories by Degree of Appropriability (7 = highest degree of appropriability)	Relative Rank of Categories by Percentage of R&D-Active Participants (7 = highest percentage of R&D activity)
1	1	4
2	7	3
3	4	6
4	2	2
5	3	1
6	5	7
7	6	5

Note: Spearman r_s = 0.32. Correlation coefficient is not significant at a conventional level.

Managers' Perceptions of the National Cooperative Research Act

As will be discussed in detail in the next chapter, in 1985 we undertook an extensive survey of R&D-active manufacturing firms in an effort to document the extent and nature of cooperative research activity. As part of that exercise, we asked the R&D vice-presidents from ninety-two firms, sixty-two of which are active in cooperative research ventures, two questions: "In your opinion, has or will the National Cooperative Research Act of 1984 affect your company's research activity (a) to a large extent, (b) to a small extent, (c) or not at all?" Our second question followed, "In your opinion, has or will the act affect the extent of cooperative research activity in your industry (a) to a large extent, (b) to a small extent, (c) or not at all?"

The executives' responses are tabulated in table 3–13. Without question, the initial perception of R&D vice-presidents, in cooperative research–active firms as well as in other firms, is clear. There is no expectation, as of 1985, that this act will significantly affect the nature of industrial research activity. We speculate in the following chapter why these research leaders may hold such an opinion.

Table 3–13
R&D Vice-Presidents' Perception of the National Cooperative Research Act
"In your opinion, has or will the National Cooperative Research Act affect your company's research activity?"

	n = 92	n = 62
To a large extent	0%	0%
To a small extent	23%	31%
Not at all	77%	69%
Total	100%	100%

"In your opinion, has or will this act affect the extent of cooperative research in your industry?"

	n = 92	n = 62
To a large extent	0%	0%
To a small extent	17%	19%
Not at all	83%	81%
Total	100%	100%

Concluding Statement

Although an inspection of the *Federal Register* filings does provide a useful overview of the types of formal cooperative relationships being undertaken in the corporate economy, the information contained therein is not a useful cynosure for a thorough understanding and assessment of the myriad aspects of cooperative research. To gain a fuller understanding, survey data were gathered on the topic, as discussed in the remaining chapters of this book.

4
Factors Affecting Cooperative Research Activities

I t is apparent from the analysis in the latter part of Chapter 3 that not enough information can be gleaned from the *Federal Register* filings regarding the causes and consequences of cooperative research endeavors. Thus, in an effort to obtain a richer empirical understanding of this important topic, a survey questionnaire was administered to a sample of R&D-active firms in the U.S. manufacturing sector.

The Survey-Based Data Set

As mentioned in the Acknowledgments at the beginning of this book, much of the material presented here is based on information obtained through mail and telephone surveys, as well as site visits, sponsored by the National Science Foundation, Division of Policy Research Analysis. In 1985, a random sample of 436 manufacturing firms, stratified by industry, was selected from the R&D Scoreboard in *Business Week*. These firms were selected to receive a mail survey related to their involvement in cooperative research. After pretesting the survey instrument, it was mailed in late 1985, and a follow-up mail/telephone survey was done in early 1986. A complete set of information (described later) was obtained from a total of 92 firms. This sample of 92 firms represents a 21 percent response rate.

Many of the surveyed firms may not have responded to the survey request for several reasons. Perhaps, they were not active in cooperative research efforts at that time, and thus the focus of the questionnaire was not relevant in their opinion. Furthermore, many firms have a corporate policy not to respond to surveys. Although a 21 percent response rate is on a par with the experiences of other researchers in both the social sciences and business-related disciplines, perhaps a higher rate could have been achieved if the population of surveyed firms were known beforehand to be active in cooperative research (or if the topic matter was not viewed as vital to these R&D-active firms' competitive strategies and thus was not treated as proprietary information). Unfortunately, at the time of the survey, virtually no economic studies had been conducted on this topic. Therefore, the population could not have been tailored more precisely. In fact, one purpose of the survey research format was to obtain a preliminary notion of the extent to which cooperation in research characterizes the overall research activities of U.S. manufacturing firms.

To investigate systematically the possibility of a response bias, we attempted to estimate, ex post facto, the probability of firm participation in this study. Specifically, we coded each of the original 436 firms dichotomously: a firm was coded with a one if it returned a usable questionnaire (as opposed to a blank or incomplete questionnaire) and zero otherwise. The independent variable selected to explain participation was firm size, as measured by each firms' 1984 sales, in billions of dollars, *SALES*.

A probit equation was estimated in order to evaluate the influence of firm size on the probability of participation. In other words, we asked whether large or small firms responded more or less frequently. The estimated probit results, with asymptotic t- statistics in parentheses, are

$$F^{-1}(P_i) = \begin{array}{cc} -1.23 & + \ 0.032 \ SALES \\ (-20.43) & (3.54) \end{array}$$

where

$$P_i = F(\alpha + \beta X_i) = F(z_i)$$

for F being the cumulative probability function, and X representing the variable *SALES*. Based on the positive algebraic sign of the probit coefficient on *SALES* and the significance of the asymptotic t- statistic on *SALES*, it appears that this sample of ninety-two participating firms is *not* a random sample from the *Business Week* population of R&D-active manufacturing firms. Rather, the sample of participants is biased toward the larger firms within that sector.

As would be expected, because larger firms are also more R&D-active, our sample of ninety-two represents the more R&D-active firms in manufacturing. As verification, the variable *SALES* was replaced in a separate regression with a variable measuring each firm's R&D expenditures, in billions of dollars, *R&D*. The corresponding probit results are

$$F^{-1}(P_i) = \begin{array}{cc} -1.21 & + \ 0.84 \ R\&D \\ (-20.36) & (2.79) \end{array}$$

These results similarly suggest that the more R&D active is a firm, the greater the probability that it responded to the survey.

Given the nature of this sample of ninety-two firms, we must offer a word of caution about generalizing from the empirical findings presented here and in the following three chapters; however, the information we obtained from on-site visits with a number of these firms leads us to believe that our conclusions may be more general than one might anticipate from these probabilities. The on-site visits (discussed in Chapter 7) were conducted after much of our analytical testing was completed. When discussing our findings with the relevant R&D managers, they offered their opinion, more times than not, that our findings closely parallel their perceptions.

An Industry Overview of Cooperative Research Activity

Selected descriptive statistics for the sample of ninety-two firms are reported in table 4–1. The mean size firm in this sample had sales in 1984 of $4,560.7 million, and the mean R&D budget was $114.8 million. A relatively wide range of firm sizes and levels of R&D spending is accounted for by this sample, reflecting primarily the cross-industry distribution of the participating firms. As a whole, just over 25 percent of all company-financed R&D within manufacturing is represented by this group of ninety-two firms.

The ninety-two firms represent sixteen of the twenty two-digit SIC industries within the manufacturing sector. The distribution of participating firms across two-digit industries is shown in table 4–2. The greatest number of participants came from the chemicals and allied products (SIC 28), machinery, except electrical (SIC 35), and electric and electronic equipment (SIC 36) industries. Tobacco products (SIC 21), apparel and other textile products (SIC 23), lumber and wood products (SIC 24), and furniture and fixtures (SIC 25) are not represented.

Table 4–1
Descriptive Statistics for the Survey Sample of Firms
(n = 92)

Variable	Mean	Standard Deviation
Sales	4,560.7	13,086.1
R&D Expenditures	114.8	384.5

Note: Variables are measured in $ millions

Table 4–2
Distribution of Sample Firms, by Two-Digit SIC Industry

SIC Code	Industry	n
20	Food and kindred products	6
21	Tobacco products	0
22	Textile mill products	1
23	Apparel and other textile products	0
24	Lumber and wood products	0
25	Furniture and fixtures	0
26	Paper and allied products	4
27	Printing and publishing	1
28	Chemicals and allied products	15
29	Petroleum and coal products	7
30	Rubber and miscellaneous plastic products	1
31	Leather and leather products	1
32	Stone, clay, and glass products	3
33	Primary metal industries	3
34	Fabricated metal products	4
35	Machinery, except electrical	14
36	Electric and electronic equipment	16
37	Transportation equipment	8
38	Instruments and related products	6
39	Miscellaneous manufacturing	2
	Total	92

Of the ninety-two firms responding, sixty-two reported that they were involved to some degree in cooperative research in 1984. *Cooperative research* was defined by us (this definition evolved from related research and pretesting information) to be *any formal or informal relationship among firms for the purpose of conducting research.* This definition was constrained to include consortia arrangements but *not* university-based research. As such, this definition is broader than an RJV (with equity distribution) and it encompasses the CRVs discussed in the preceding chapter. (As discussed later in this chapter and those that follow, data were gathered on cooperative research activities for 1983, 1984, and estimations for 1985; however, only a subset of these sixty-two firms responded to the questions pertaining to 1983 and estimated 1985 activities.)

The distribution of the sixty-two cooperative research–active firms is shown in table 4–3, by two-digit SIC industry. The industries most heavily represented are chemicals (SIC 28) with eight firms; petroleum and coal products (SIC 29) with seven firms; machinery (SIC 35) with ten firms; and

Table 4–3
Distribution of Cooperative Research–Active Firms, by Two-Digit SIC
Industry

SIC Code	Industry	n
20	Food and kindred products	5
21	Tobacco products	NA
22	Textile mill products	1
23	Apparel and other textile products	NA
24	Lumber and wood products	NA
25	Furniture and fixtures	NA
26	Paper and allied products	2
27	Printing and publishing	0
28	Chemicals and allied products	8
29	Petroleum and coal products	7
30	Rubber and miscellaneous plastic products	1
31	Leather and leather products	0
32	Stone, clay, and glass products	2
33	Primary metal industries	2
34	Fabricated metal products	3
35	Machinery, except electrical	10
36	Electric and electronic equipment	10
37	Transportation equipment	5
38	Instruments and related products	4
39	Miscellaneous manufacturing	2
	Total	62

electric and electronic equipment (SIC 36) also with ten firms. In addition
to the four industries in table 4–2 for which no firms are represented, the
printing and publishing industry (SIC 27) and the leather products industry
(SIC 31) are not actively involved in cooperative research.

A comparison of tables 4–2 and 4–3 is presented in table 4–4, listing
the percentages of the ninety-two responding firms engaged in cooperative
research by two-digit industry. Of the five industry groupings with the
largest number of firms responding to the survey—SICs 28, 29, 35, 36, and
38—the variation in the reported percentages is noticeable. Only 53 percent of the responding firms in the chemicals industry engaged in cooperative research in 1984, whereas 100 percent did so in the petroleum
industry. As we discuss in Chapter 5, the strategic motivation for undertaking research cooperatively varies across industry. Perhaps this explains the
interindustry variation noted in table 4–4.

Table 4–5 illustrates, on an industry basis, the actual number of coop-

Table 4–4
Distribution of Percentage of Firms Engaged in Cooperative Research Activity, by Two-Digit SIC Industry

SIC Code	Industry	Percentage
20	Food and kindred products	0.83
21	Tobacco products	NA
22	Textile mill products	1.00
23	Apparel and other textile products	NA
24	Lumber and wood products	NA
25	Furniture and fixtures	NA
26	Paper and allied products	0.50
27	Printing and publishing	0.00
28	Chemicals and allied products	0.53
29	Petroleum and coal products	1.00
30	Rubber and miscellaneous plastic products	1.00
31	Leather and leather products	0.00
32	Stone, clay, and glass products	0.67
33	Primary metal industries	0.67
34	Fabricated metal products	0.75
35	Machinery, except electrical	0.71
36	Electric and electronic equipment	0.63
37	Transportation equipment	0.63
38	Instruments and related products	0.67
39	Miscellaneous manufacturing	1.00

erative research projects undertaken by the subsample of sixty-two firms. These projects are reported in total and according to whether the cooperative arrangement was formal or informal. Nearly 90 percent of the reported 446 projects were informal cooperative arrangements. Given this finding, as well as anecdotal evidence that informal agreements dominate cooperative research partnerships, it is not surprising that our earlier analysis of the *Federal Register* filings was limited in scope.

From table 4–5 we see that sixty-two cooperative research–active firms undertook 446 separate projects with other firms. Extrapolating from this sample on the basis of the size distribution of these sixty-two firms and the thirty noncooperating firms, we project that 6,641 cooperative research projects took place in 1984 within firms in the manufacturing sector. The distribution of these projects, by industry, is shown in table 4–6. As before, the chemicals industry (SIC 28) is very active in cooperative research. But also, cooperation appears to be a significant endeavor in the transportation equipment industry (SIC 37). If the estimated 1985 values are used (the

Table 4–5
Distribution of Number of Cooperative Research Projects, by Two-Digit
SIC Industry (n = 62)

| SIC Code | Industry | Number of Projects | | |
		Informal	Formal	Total
20	Food and kindred products	20	2	22
21	Tobacco products	NA	NA	NA
22	Textile mill products	6	0	6
23	Apparel and other textile products	NA	NA	NA
24	Lumber and wood products	NA	NA	NA
25	Furniture and fixtures	NA	NA	NA
26	Paper and allied products	40	3	43
27	Printing and publishing	0	0	0
28	Chemicals and allied products	95	14	109
29	Petroleum and coal products	59	6	65
30	Rubber and miscellaneous plastic products	8	1	9
31	Leather and leather products	0	0	0
32	Stone, clay, and glass products	20	1	21
33	Primary metal industries	3	0	3
34	Fabricated metal products	2	2	4
35	Machinery, except electrical	52	9	61
36	Electric and electronic equipment	62	13	75
37	Transportation equipment	11	4	15
38	Instruments and related products	7	1	8
39	Miscellaneous manufacturing	5	0	5
	Total	390	56	446

sample size reduces from sixty-two to fifty-four), the number of projects in manufacturing increases to 8,213—a 23.7 percent increase between the two years.

The information in table 4–7 relates to the number of cooperative research projects undertaken per firm during 1984. The entries in this table come from those in table 4–5, divided by those in table 4–3. The range of cooperative research projects undertaken per firm is also large: 21.5 cooperative research projects per firm in the paper industry to less than 2 per firm in the metals industries. The mean number of cooperative research projects per firm is 7.2.

It is interesting to note from table 4–7 and table 4–4 that all seven petroleum firms in the sample of ninety-two were engaged in cooperative research, but just over one-half of the fifteen firms in the chemicals industry are similarly characterized. However, the number of cooperative research

Table 4–6
Projected Number of Cooperative Research Projects, by Two-Digit SIC Industry

SIC Code	Industry	Number of Projects
20	Food and kindred products	119
21	Tobacco products	NA
22	Textile mill products	119
23	Apparel and other textile products	NA
24	Lumber and wood products	NA
25	Furniture and fixtures	NA
26	Paper and allied products	590
27	Printing and publishing	0
28	Chemicals and allied products	1,816
29	Petroleum and coal products	615
30	Rubber and miscellaneous plastic products	71
31	Leather and leather products	0
32	Stone, clay, and glass products	244
33	Primary metal industries	54
34	Fabricated metal products	165
35	Machinery, except electrical	624
36	Electric and electronic equipment	890
37	Transportation equipment	1,017
38	Instruments and related products	151
39	Miscellaneous manufacturing	166
	Total	6,641

projects per firm is 46 percent greater in chemicals than petroleum: 13.6 percent compared to 9.3 percent. Similar comparisons are obvious upon inspection of these data.

It is likely to be the case that cooperative research activity cannot accurately be compared across industries on an individual project basis. The nature (scale as well as scope) of such research arrangements varies so much across industries (or even across lines of business) that to undertake such an exercise would invite invidious comparisons. Thus, we view the information in table 4–7 as a description of only one aspect of such activity.

Interindustry Differences in Cooperative Research Activity

Perhaps a more meaningful interindustry comparison of cooperative research activity can be made in terms of the investment intensity characteriz-

Table 4–7
Distribution of Cooperative Research Projects per Firm, by Two-Digit SIC Industry (n = 62)

SIC Code	Industry	Cooperative Research Projects per Firm
20	Food and kindred products	4.4
21	Tobacco products	NA
22	Textile mill products	6.0
23	Apparel and other textile products	NA
24	Lumber and wood products	NA
25	Furniture and fixtures	NA
26	Paper and allied products	21.5
27	Printing and publishing	0
28	Chemicals and allied products	13.6
29	Petroleum and coal products	9.3
30	Rubber and miscellaneous plastic products	9.0
31	Leather and leather products	0
32	Stone, clay, and glass products	10.5
33	Primary metal industries	1.5
34	Fabricated metal products	1.3
35	Machinery, except electrical	6.1
36	Electric and electronic equipment	7.5
37	Transportation equipment	3.0
38	Instruments and related products	2.0
39	Miscellaneous manufacturing	2.5
	Mean	7.2

ing that research form. Each of the sixty-two cooperative research–active firms was asked as part of the survey, what percentage of their company-financed R&D was allocated to cooperative research activity in 1984. For the sixty-two firms as a group, the mean percentage is 0.073, with a standard deviation of 0.065. These percentages are reported in table 4–8, by two-digit industry. Again, there is considerable variation in these data. The range is 13.8 percent in miscellaneous manufacturing to 2.3 percent in the paper industry to zero percent in both the printing and the leather industries.

A casual inspection of the data in table 4–8 suggests that cooperative research is relatively more important, as evidenced by the percent of R&D invested in that activity, in the more technologically advanced industries within manufacturing than in other industries. Those industries that are more R&D-active, in general, are also those allocating a larger percentage of their R&D budget to cooperative arrangements.

Table 4–8

Distribution of the Percentage of Company-Financed R&D Allocated to Cooperative Research by Cooperative Research–Active Firms, by Two-Digit SIC Industry

SIC Code	Industry	Percentage
20	Food and kindred products	.058
21	Tobacco products	NA
22	Textile mill products	.026
23	Apparel and other textile products	NA
24	Lumber and wood products	NA
25	Furniture and fixtures	NA
26	Paper and allied products	.023
27	Printing and publishing	0
28	Chemicals and allied products	.073
29	Petroleum and coal products	.063
30	Rubber and miscellaneous plastic products	.055
31	Leather and leather products	0
32	Stone, clay, and glass products	.051
33	Primary metal industries	.040
34	Fabricated metal products	.062
35	Machinery, except electrical	.068
36	Electric and electronic equipment	.088
37	Transportation equipment	.081
38	Instruments and related products	.121
39	Miscellaneous manufacturing	.138
	Mean	.073

We correlated the percentages reported in table 4–8 (less SIC 39 for lack of reliable companion data) with company-funded R&D as a percent of industry sales for 1984. The latter industry series comes from unpublished sources at the National Science Foundation. The simple correlation coefficient is 0.84, and it is highly significant. Thus, it appears to be the case that the more research-active the industry, the greater is the proportion of those funds allocated to cooperative endeavors.

We posited in Chapters 1 and 2 and in *Strategies for Technology-Based Competition: Meeting the New Global Challenge,* that cooperative research is a technology-based strategic response to global competition and to the associated shortened life cycle. Although there are no theoretical models or empirical studies to use as a bench mark for this hypothesis, the popular press is replete with anecdotal evidence to support this view. Some of that material was quoted in the previous chapters. Still, it remains an empirical issue to substantiate our prescription for increased cooperation as an effective competitive strategy.

As an initial inquiry, in figure 4–1, we plotted, by two-digit SIC industry, the percentage of company-financed R&D allocated to cooperative research, *CRPCT*, against the share of total domestic sales from imports—a measure of foreign competition, *FCOMP*. The import shares for 1983 (which implicitly assumes a one-year lag in response) are ratios of the two-digit SIC industry imports divided by the value of shipments plus imports less exports. Data on import and exports come from the International Trade Commission and data on shipments come from the Bureau of Industrial Economics.

No clear pattern can be discerned in figure 4–1. At least at the two-digit level of analysis, the percentage of industry R&D allocated to cooperation is no greater in industries facing relatively more intense foreign competition. The correlation coefficient is 0.13, and it is not significant at a conventional level. When only cooperative research–active industries are considered—that is, when the printing and leather industries are excluded—the correlation coefficient is 0.70, and it is highly significant. Perhaps a firm-level analysis will reveal more on these interesting points.[1]

Interfirm Differences in Cooperative Research Activity

The Analytical Framework

Our sample of ninety-two R&D active firms contains sixty-two firms active in cooperative research and thirty non-cooperative research–active firms, which raises an interesting question: What economic factors explain this observed interfirm variation in cooperative research activity? Note that this variation contains information on two phenomena: the difference between firms that cooperate versus those that do not, and the difference between the percentage of R&D allocated to cooperative research activities among the sixty-two cooperating firms.

An analysis of the economics literature indicates that interfirm differences in cooperative research activity have not been analyzed previously in any meaningful detail. One exception is our study of innovative behavior in the video display terminal (VDT) industry. Our findings that relate specifically to cooperative research in that industry are presented in the appendix to this chapter.[2]

In the following empirical analyses, we focus on three variables that are hypothesized to affect the decision to engage in cooperative research activity: foreign competition, firm profitability, and firm market power. The

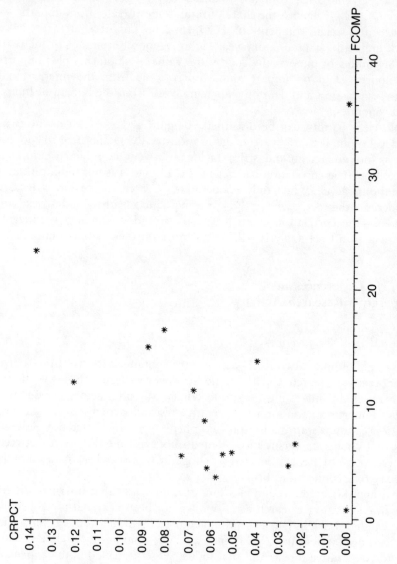

Figure 4–1. Relationship between Cooperative Research Activity and Foreign Competition, by Two-Digit SIC Industry

underlying premise for investigating the influence of foreign competition has been noted in the previous chapters. The justification for the latter two variables' assumed influence on cooperative research behavior is based on the economics literature, which emphasizes the relationship between these two variables on innovation per se. Those arguments are summarized later. Regarding the influence of profitability and market power on interfirm differences in cooperative research, there is a literature upon which hypotheses can be formed.

Cooperative research, like any form of research, involves risk and uncertainty. As such, cooperative research endeavors generally require substantial and often prolonged financial support. External funding for such undertakings is often difficult to obtain by firms engaged in the more traditional internal R&D endeavors and may be virtually nonexistent for those proposing cooperative ventures (or other activities that are viewed, justifiably or not, by the market as uncertain and risk-intensive). Thus, internal sources of financing must be available for nearly any research undertaking of this type.

It has been argued that the R&D-to-profits relationship is stronger in some types of firms than in others. Theoretical analyses related to this topic conclude that marginal firms (that is, those engaged in "risky" R&D ventures) face an active self-financing constraint. Thus, current profits are a necessary condition for their R&D spending. Established firms doing the more "routine" product development types of innovative activities will not be as constrained by the availability of cash and will not require high current cash flows to finance their research programs.[3] Related empirical research supports this generalization. Given this, and the fact that cooperative research is likely to be oriented toward the basic or generic end of an R&D spectrum (this point is developed in greater detail in Chapter 6), it follows that firm profitability should be a prerequisite for firms to be active in that form of research.

However, a countervailing argument is also possible. Firms with low or declining profits may feel pressure to innovate in order to remain competitive.[4] If so, increased R&D is a reasonable method for pursuing such a strategy. And, because of waning profitability, cooperative research may be the preferred organizational arrangement for such undertakings owing to the ability of the participants to share costs. So, then, firm profitability and involvement in cooperative research should be inversely related to each other.

Thus, the theoretical literature in economics related to the R&D-to-profits relationship is contradictory, although the empirical literature suggests a positive relationship between the two variables. It remains an empirical question, then, as to whether this same positive relationship also holds for cooperative research.

Regarding market power, one of the most frequently investigated topics in the industrial organization literature is the relationship between market power and innovative activity. Specifically, is it the possession of, or rather the quest for, market power that stimulates innovation? The so-called Schumpeterian position is that market dominance is an important determinant of innovation. Since cooperative research has a greater degree of "publicness" than internal R&D (see Chapter 6), by design, firms who have the ability to internalize the benefits from shared knowledge are, following Schumpeter, more likely to invest in it than would other firms. However, others have demonstrated that the relationship between innovation (R&D investments) and market power can not be predicted unambiguously from economic theory. The empirical evidence is also mixed.[5] Thus, the relationship between involvement in cooperative research and market power is an empirical issue as well.

The Statistical Analysis

The model hypothesized to explain interfirm differences in cooperative research activity can be written in functional form as

$$CRPCT = f(FCOMP, PROFIT, MKTPOW)$$

The dependent variable, *CRPCT*, represents the percentage of each firm's R&D budget for 1984 allocated to cooperative research activities (as we previously defined that term). *FCOMP* represents the extent of foreign competition that the firm faces. *PROFIT* represents the profitability of each firm. The variable *MKTPOW* approximates the degree of market power associated with each firm's activities.

The percentage of company-financed R&D allocated to cooperative research activity was obtained from our survey. As shown in table 4–9, the mean value for *CRPCT* for the entire sample of ninety-two firms is 0.049, with a standard deviation of 0.063. For the sixty-two cooperative research–active firms, the mean value increases to 7.3 percent and the standard deviation is virtually unchanged, as expected. As previously stated, these data relate to 1984.

The extent to which each firm is affected by foreign competition is measured by the import share associated with the three-digit SIC industry in which the firm produces. A three-digit classification was deemed better able to capture the multiline of business activity of these firms, than a four-digit industry classification. The variable *FCOMP* was constructed as the ratio of industry imports divided by the value of industry shipments plus imports less exports. As at the two-digit level discussed earlier, data on imports and exports come from the International Trade Commission and

Table 4–9
Descriptive Statistics on the Primary Data

Variable	n = 92	n = 62	n = 30
CRPCT:			
Mean	0.049	0.073	0.00
Standard deviation	0.063	0.065	NA
FCOMP:			
Mean	11.72	13.18	8.70
Standard deviation	10.14	10.23	9.41
PROFIT:			
Mean	0.026	0.019	0.040
Standard deviation	0.039	0.029	0.051
WCR:			
Mean	0.434	0.434	0.433
Standard deviation	0.179	0.186	0.167
WMS:			
Mean	0.038	0.046	0.020
Standard deviation	0.085	0.099	0.034

data on shipments come from the Bureau of Industrial Economics. As reported in table 4–9, the mean value of *FCOMP* is 11.72 for the entire sample, with a standard deviation of 10.14. The mean value is about 50 percent larger for the subsample of sixty-two cooperating firms, 13.18, compared to the subsample of thirty noncooperating firms, 8.70. Casually interpreted, cooperative research–active firms face a greater degree of foreign competition than do non-cooperative research–active firms. As discussed later, this casual interpretation is not at odds with the relationship between the percentage of R&D allocated to cooperation and the extent of foreign competition at the two-digit level, shown in figure 4–1.

The profitability of each firm, *PROFIT*, is measured as the ratio of 1984 profits to sales, as reported in *Business Week*. Referring to the descriptive statistics in table 4–9, the mean value of this ratio is 2.6 percent for the entire sample of ninety-two firms, 1.9 percent for the subsample of sixty-two cooperating firms and 4.0 percent for the subsample of thirty firms that are not active in cooperative research. Casually interpreted, it appears that, on average, cooperating firms are less profitable than the noncooperating firms in this sample of ninety-two. Standard deviations are also reported in the table.

Market power is a concept in economics that has a distinct meaning for theoretical analyses but is rather ellusive when it comes to empirical inquiries. Following others, we *approximate* market power using two variables: a weighted four-firm SIC industry concentration ratio, *WCR*, and a weighted market share variable for each firm, *WMS*.

As part of our survey, each firm was asked to allocate its 1984 sales across its various lines of business. For each firm, each line of business was assigned a four-digit SIC industry concentration ratio.[6] Then, each concentration ratio was weighted by the relative percentage of each firm's total sales in order to construct a firm-specific variable, *WRC*. In a similar fashion, each firm's share of total industry sales was calculated by line of business and then weighted by the relevant percentage of total sales.

Referring again to table 4–9, there is no apparent difference between the two subsamples in the mean value of *WCR*, and the standard deviations differ very little. Casually interpreted, cooperation is not an industry-specific phenomenon as reflected in these industry concentration ratios. However, the mean value of the weighted market share variable is over twice as large for the subsample of cooperative research–active firms as for the subsample of thirty firms who do not cooperate. The mean values are, respectively, 0.046 and 0.020. Of course, as noted in the table, there is significantly greater variation in these market share values among the subsample of sixty-two firms than among the subsample of thirty firms.

Because the dependent variable in this analysis, *CRPCT*, is truncated at zero, a Tobit model was selected to analyze interfirm differences in cooperative research spending as a percentage of total R&D. The relevant Tobit model is

$$y_i = \begin{cases} y_i^* & \text{for } y_i^* > \text{zero} \\ \text{zero} & \text{for } y_i \leq \text{zero} \end{cases} \tag{4.1}$$

where y_i refers to the dependent variable *CRPCT* and where

$$y_i^* = \mathbf{X}_i \, \beta + \epsilon$$

for $E(\epsilon_i) = \text{zero}$ and $\text{Var}(\epsilon_i) = \sigma^2$, using matrix notation. The vector $\mathbf{X}_i$ contains the four independent variables *FCOMP*, *PROFIT*, *WCR*, *WMS*, and a constant.

In the Tobit model, the variable y_i^* can be thought of as an unobserved variable representing cooperative research potential. If y_i^* is positive, it is observed, but if y_i^* is less than or equal to zero we observe that the firm has no cooperative R&D expenditures. The Tobit coefficients from equation (4.1) are estimated by maximum likelihood and presented in table 4–10. Ordinary least-squares estimates for the sample of ninety-two firms are presented in table 4–11 for comparison.

Based on significance levels repeated in table 4–10, the most important variable explaining cooperative research activity is the extent to which each firm faces foreign competition. The Tobit coefficient on *FCOMP* is

Table 4–10
Tobit Estimates Based on Equation (4.1) (ratio of $\hat{\beta}/s_{\hat{\beta}}$ in parentheses: n = 92)

Independent Variable	Coefficient
FCOMP	0.0039
	(5.48)**
PROFIT	−0.160
	(−0.80)
WCR	0.046
	(1.08)
WMS	0.187
	(2.27)*
Constant	0.035
	(−1.82)
Standard error	0.061
χ^2_4	21.31**

*Significant at .05 level.
**Significant at .01 level.

positive and highly significant. This finding is consistent with our hypothesis that cooperative research is a technology-based response to competition in world markets, although it *appears* to contradict the overall correlation evidence at the two-digit level in figure 4–1. It does not, however, contradict the evidence when the two noncooperating industries are deleted.

Table 4–11
Ordinary Least-Squares Regression Results Based on Equation (4.1) (t-statistics in parentheses)

Independent Variable	n = 92
FCOMP	0.003
	(6.13)**
PROFIT	0.010
	(0.08)
WCR	0.062
	(2.05)*
WMS	0.168
	(2.68)**
Constant	−0.022
	(−1.61)
R2	0.46
F-level	18.63**

*Significant at .05 level.
**Significant at .01 level.

The Tobit coefficient on *PROFIT* is negative but insignificant. Profitability is not an important factor in explaining interfirm differences in cooperative research activity, other things held constant, although the descriptive statistics in table 4–9 suggest that it may be important. Of the two so-called market power variables considered, only *WMS* is significant. Firms that dominate their industry (that is, those with larger market shares) are more likely to engage in cooperative research than are their domestic competitors. Industry concentration, as measured by the variable *WCR*, does not have a significant influence on explaining cooperative research behavior. These two conclusions were suggested by the descriptive data in table 4–9.

Although ordinary least-squares (OLS) analysis is statistically inappropriate when the dependent variable is truncated, as it is here, it still provides a useful bench mark for comparisons. The OLS results in table 4–11 reveal a similar behavioral pattern. The only exception is the significance of *WCR* in the OLS model.

Twelve two-digit industry dummy variables were included in another version of equation (4.1), but as a group these variables were not significant and thus they were deleted.[7] In other words, the interindustry variation in *CRPCT* in table 4–8 unexplained by variation in the independent variables is not an industry phenomenon. Similarly, the possibility of nonlinear relationships between the dependent variable and the two market power variables were considered, but in no alternative version of equation (4.1) could a nonlinear effect be determined.

In order to investigate in even greater detail the implications of the Tobit results in table 4–10, a decomposition technique was employed. Specifically, using the notation from equation (4.1):

$$\partial E(y)/\partial X_j = [F(z) \, (\partial E(y^*)/\partial X_j)] + [E(y^*) \, (\partial F(z)/\partial X_j)] \qquad (4.2)$$

where the change in the expected value of y, $E(y)$, with respect to a change in one of the independent variables, X_j, has two distinct parts, as bracketed. The term in the first bracketed expression is the change in the expected value of y, $E(y^*)$, by firms above the limit ($y_i^* > $ zero) weighted by the probability of being above the limit, $F(z)$; and the term in the second bracketed expression is the change in the probability of being above the limit weighted by the expected value of y above the limit.[8] That is,

$E(y)$ = the expected value of y;

$E(y^*)$ = the expected value of y^* previously defined in equation (4.1);

$\partial E(y^*)/\partial X_j$ = the change in the expected value of y^* for a change in X_j;

$F(z)$ = the cumulative normal distribution function, or the probability of being above the limit;

$\partial F(z)/\partial X_j$ = the change in the probability of being above the limit for a change in X_j.

The values of the terms in equation (4.2), based on the analysis underlying the results presented in table 4–10, are reported in table 4–12.

Since y is the percentage of firm R&D allocated to cooperative research activities, and thus zero $\leq y \geq 1$, and since zero $\leq F(z) \leq 1$, then for each X_j, $[\partial E(y^*)/\partial X_j]$ may be compared numerically to $[\partial F(z)/\partial X_j]$ in order to determine the relative impact of a change in X_j on the expected value of y by firms above the limit versus the probability of being above the limit. Such a comparison of the significant independent variables is very revealing.

Increases in foreign competition, *FCOMP*, and in market share, *WMS*, have a greater impact on whether a firm decides to engage in cooperative research than on whether a cooperating firm decides to allocate a marginal dollar to such an activity. Specifically, $\partial F(z)/\partial FCOMP > \partial E(y^*)/\partial FCOMP$, and similarly for the market share variable, WMS. This is seen from the information in table 4–12. Alternatively stated, the extent of foreign competition on domestic markets seems to spur firms into cooperation more so than to provide an incentive for those who already cooperate to do more of the same. This finding is not at odds with the casual interpretation from table 4–9 that foreign competition is greater among those firms that cooperate ($n = 62$) compared with those who do not ($n = 30$). Similarly, this finding is not at odds with our earlier interindustry analysis of a general lack of correlation between foreign competition and industry intensiveness in cooperative R&D spending ($n = 62$).

Likewise, to the extent that their market share affords firms the ability

Table 4–12
Calculated Values of the Components of the Determinants of Cooperative Research

X_j	$\partial E(y)/\partial X_j$	$\partial E(y^*)/\partial X_j$	$\partial F(z)/\partial X_j$
FCOMP	0.00282	0.00199	0.02201
PROFIT	−0.11395	−0.08037	−0.89032
WCR	0.03241	0.02286	0.25324
WMS	0.13309	0.09387	1.03987

Note: z = 0.55362 evaluated as the mean of all X_js.
$F(z)$ = 0.71008
$E(y)$ = 0.04536
$E(y^*)$ = 0.06389

to appropriate technical knowledge, that ability is relatively more critical for their decision to engage in cooperative research. But once that initial decision is made, additional market power has less effect on the allocation of a marginal R&D dollar to cooperation.

This decomposition of the Tobit results in table 4–10 leads to one additional statistical inference. If both sides of equation (4.2) are divided by $F(z)\beta_j$, then

$$1 = \left[1 - \frac{zf(z)}{F(z)} - \frac{f(z)^2}{F(z)^2} \right] + \left[\frac{E(y^*)(\partial F(z)/\partial X_j)}{F(z)\beta_j} \right] \quad (4.3)$$

where $f(z)$ is the unit normal density function. The first bracketed expression is generally referred to as *fraction*, and in this case it equals 0.50083. The value of the fraction reveals that the total effect of changes in *CRPCT* from changes in *all* the independent variables is divided approximately equally between firms already engaged in cooperative research activity and those just beginning to undertake that activity.

Concluding Statement

Cooperative research appears to be an activity common to firms throughout the manufacturing sector. Although some firms devote a larger portion of their R&D budget to this activity than others, those differences are not an industry-specific phenomenon. Our analysis suggests that two principal factors influence a firm's decision to engage in cooperative research: the extent to which it faces foreign competition, and its share of the domestic market in which it participates. Although these factors have a significantly greater impact on the initial decision on whether to cooperate, they still exhibit a positive influence on firms once the decision to cooperate is made. Among cooperating firms, those facing the greatest degree of foreign competition and those that dominate their industry are engaged in cooperative research activity more intensely than are others.

While it is difficult to forecast changes in firms' market shares over time, we contend that foreign competition will continue to increase owing to an increase in the size of world markets and the trend toward technological parity among participants. As such, our analysis predicts that U.S. manufacturing firms will respond primarily by *beginning* to form strategic cooperative research alliances. Recall that our data show a 23.7 percent increase in cooperative research projects between 1984 and 1985. To re-quote Nils Wilhjelm, Denmark's minister of industry, from Chapter 1, "The individual company securing its continuous development by itself has now become history. To obtain results, it is today necessary to cooperate."

In the next chapter we explore why firms cooperate. Specifically, we investigate, using our survey subsample of sixty-two firms, the various strategic motives behind the decision to engage in cooperative research ventures.

Appendix 4A: Cooperative R&D in the Video Display Terminal Industry

The video display terminal (VDT) industry is small in terms of its contribution to Gross National Product, but it is perhaps a prototype of an important cadre of technologically progressive industries (such as solar energy, biogenetics, and microelectronics) developing with the economies of many developed nations. As such, the VDT industry is a potentially interesting industry to examine in terms of its innovative behavior. We present here the results of an exploratory study into the factors related to cooperative research activity in the VDT industry.[9]

The VDT Industry

A VDT consists of a cathode ray tube (CRT), a keyboard, information processing circuitry, and possibly embedded software. These products evolved in the early 1970s as a replacement for the teletype terminal to improve direct human interaction with computer systems. The U.S. VDT industry consisted at the time of this investigation (1982) of about 200 manufacturers with total sales in 1982 of more than 3.4 billion units, an installed base of over 6.5 million units, and a growth rate of 20 to 25 percent per year.

In 1982, the industry could be characterized briefly as follows. First, there was a high degree of seller concentration and a very low degree of buyer concentration. Second, the industry experienced rapid technological change (evidenced by a rapid introduction of new products, new product features, and expanded product capabilities). There was an intense level of R&D competition in the industry and product life cycles were, on average, less than three years long. Third, although it was relatively concentrated on the seller side (a five-firm concentration ratio of 40 percent), there were very few barriers to entry into this industry. Fourth, there appear to have been substantial barriers to survival. Innovation was occurring as a continuous stream of incremental enhancements rather than as radical technological breakthroughs—and we note that this characterization may mirror the kinds of technological changes that could be seen in the high-technology sector of this country in the decade to come. Since most innovations in this industry are either imitated quickly or not accepted in the marketplace, a sustained R&D program was required for corporate success. This reliance on an ongoing R&D agenda was especially troublesome for the smaller firms, who had successfully entered the market with an innovative product but then had to sustain this performance level over the long run in order to survive. Although innovative products were rewarded by a rapid growth in sales, efforts to exploit this demand required firms to shift financial resources into production and customer service. As a result, R&D, especially long-term R&D, suffered. When larger firms began to imitate the successful product innovations of these smaller firms by offering improved, lower-cost versions, the smaller innovative firms rapidly lost their market share, and many exited from the industry because they could not strategically direct their R&D toward newer, more innovative products.

In 1982, there were three major submarkets in the VDT industry: dumb, smart, and intelligent terminals. In 1979, dumb terminal sales accounted for 27 percent of total industry sales, with smart and intelligent terminals accounting for 58 and 15 percent, respectively. Dumb VDTs, often referred to as *glass teletypes*, possessed little, if any, internal processing capabilities. The first generation of dumb VDTs were introduced in the early 1970s and sold for between $1,000 and $2,500, depending on external features. Technological advances in the mid-1970s reducing the number of discrete components required in manufacturing, along with economies of scale in production, reduced the price of second generation units to between $400 and $500. Prices in the early 1980s were at about the same level and there appeared, at that time, to be little further potential for drastic cost reductions without a radical technological breakthrough.

In 1982, the dumb VDT segment could best be described as mature, with competition taking the form of advertising to stress product attributes. R&D activity in this submarket tended to be product-related and defensive in strategic scope. Most of the associated technology came from outside of the firm in the form of purchased components, such as CRTs and microcircuitry. Today, this segment of the industry has disappeared owing to the influence of robotic technology in the production processes of the other segments of the industry. Robotic technology has lowered the production cost in these segments to levels at which the production of dumb VDTs is no longer profitable. And, as would be expected, the market for such a product has vanished.

Smart VDTs are configured with internal circuity enabling prespecified internal processing such as line editing and data entry operations. This was a maturing market in 1982, having experienced its "shake-out" stage several years earlier. Although prices were set initially around $3,000, competition and experience in production had driven them to as low as $600 by 1982. With the advent of robotic technology into the production process, the price is less than $300 today.

Intelligent VDTs provide sufficient internal circuitry, storage, and software that sophisticated information processing can be performed locally. With the inclusion of a compiler or interpreter, a machine's local capabilities can be revised or extended simply by acquiring compatible software packages. In 1982, this was an immature industry with evolving technologies and differing product prices (then $2,500 to $8,000 depending on features), but the industry was just entering its growth phase. As is well known, personal computers directly confronted the growth of this industry, and today's prices are in the range of $300 to $400. The evolutionary phenomenon being observed is the merger of personal computers and intelligent VDTs into workstations. The workstation industry is today beginning its growth stage.

Cooperative Research Activity in the VDT Industry

To investigate the extent and nature of cooperative research activity in this industry, 221 organizations believed to have been associated with the VDT industry were contacted in 1981. Because there was no complete listing of industry members, this grouping was collected primarily from product announcements and advertisements. Research instruments were sent in 1982 to those 78 organizations that were, in fact, active in this industry and that agreed to participate in the research project. Usable responses were ultimately received from 34 of these firms. Firms *not* included within this sample of 34 organizations were those who did not manufacture VDTs, those no longer in business, those no longer manufacturing VDTs, those reluctant to release the requested survey data, and those unable to provide accurately the requested survey data. Firms unable to provide the survey data generally fell into one of two categories: large diversified manufacturers who organized their R&D around technologies rather than products (and hence were unable to isolate VDT R&D activities), and small manufacturers who simply had not gathered data in a format compatible with ours. IBM's VDT activities, although in 1982 they accounted for nearly 20 percent of industry sales, are conspicuously absent. IBM, as well as other computer industry giants, were included in the initial set of surveyed firms.

Although the number of firms the sample investigated is small, they accounted for 60 percent of 1981 industry sales and include a wide range of alternatively sized firms as well as a wide range of R&D spending patterns. Each of the three industry submarkets is well represented; however, rarely did any one firm produce in each of the three submarkets. Nine of the organizations specialized completely in a single submarket, and the remainder of firms had the majority of their sales in either the dumb-smart submarket or in the intelligent submarket. Despite the obvious limitations of employing such a limited sample of manufacturing firms, there is the advantage of tighter control of contextual and environmental factors, especially when there are contrasting innovative activities.

From each firm, we obtained information relating to its expenditures on total R&D and on cooperative research projects (CRP) undertaken in 1982. Surprisingly, each of the thirty-four firms had been involved in at least one joint research activity, formal or informal, during that year. However, the majority of innovative activity was conducted internally. As a sample, the firms reported that eighty-four of the research projects completed in 1982 were conducted in-house and funded solely from internal R&D.

In order to explain interfirm differences in the extent of cooperation, two variables were focused upon. The first explanatory variable was the size of the firm. Firm size was quantified by the organization's gross VDT sales in that year, *SALES*. As discussed in the body of Chapter 4, a large literature in economics suggests that size is an important correlate with innovativeness, as measured by R&D spending in total or by type. Also included as an explanatory factor is the percent of each VDT organization's sales coming from each of the industry submarkets. This variable, *MARKET*, was measured as the fraction (between zero and 1) of sales in the intelligent terminal market. By so measuring this variable, we are assuming that the dumb and smart terminal submarkets are innovatively the same. It is expected that more cooperative research would take place in the intelligent terminal market where no dominant design had yet emerged, competition was still in terms of the continued introduction of successful technology-based innovations, and the speed of introduction and the ability to share research costs was perceived to render an important competitive advantage.

The following regression model was estimated using ordinary-least squares analysis:

$$\ln CRP = \beta_0 + \beta_1 \ln SALES + \beta_2 MARKET + \epsilon$$

where ϵ is a random error term assumed to obey all of the classical assumptions.

The estimated regression coefficient on $\ln SALES$ is 0.35. Relevant t-tests indicate that this estimated elasticity is not significantly different from zero ($t = 1.91$), but it is significantly less than unity ($t = -3.49$). This finding implies that larger firms in this industry do spend more on cooperative research ventures than smaller firms but not proportionally more relative to their size. In contrast, when the size elasticity of total R&D spending was computed from an alternative regression model, the elasticity was 0.54. This estimated coefficient is significantly greater than zero ($t = 4.61$) but also significantly less than unity ($t = -3.86$).

The estimated coefficient on the variable *MARKET* is 1.99, and it is significantly different from zero at the 0.05 level ($t = 2.34$). Apparently, firms specializing in the production of intelligent VDTs are, holding size constant, more reliant on cooperative research activity to enhance their competitive position than are firms in the other segments of the industry, as expected.

It appears, therefore, that cooperative research is a technology-based, competitive strategy practiced by all firms in our sample from the VDT industry; some more than others. Those for whom cooperative research is more important are those who face the most rapidly changing technology— producers of intelligent VDTs.

It is important to also note that cooperative research, although practiced primarily on an informal basis in this industry as in manufacturing as a whole (see table 4–5), is a well-established research-related policy. It seems to have evolved naturally as a response to competition well before the beginning of the dialogue associated with the passage of the National Cooperative Research Act.

5
Cooperative Research as a Competitive Strategy

The concepts that underlie the notion of competitive strategy are well known to students of economics and the management sciences. Rivalry implies the adoption of alternative strategies in pursuit of profits or some other objective. Such strategies include, but are not limited to, alternative pricing behavior, patterns of diversification, and vertical integration. Surprisingly, however, very little is formally known about technology-based strategies in general or about cooperative research strategies, in particular. What is known comes instinctively to managers. As Roland W. Schmitt, senior vice-president and chief scientist at General Electric Company recently noted:

> The need for [technical] cooperation arises from several situations. One may find an opportunity that fits the business strategy, but lack the needed technical capabilities. One may recognize that cooperation permits lower costs of development than does unilateral action. Or there may be complementary capabilities in a partner that allow one to extend product scope and markets beyond those that could be addressed alone.[1]

The purpose of this chapter is twofold: one, to analyze the extent—the scale as well as the scope—to which cooperative research activities are used to pursue various competitive strategies; and two, to identify factors related to firms' choices of strategies.

Technology-Based Competitive Strategies

Firms within technologically progressive industries can be classified into one of two broad categories depending on whether their dominant technology-based competitive strategy is *innovative* or *imitative*.[2] Although most firms, especially those within the manufacturing sectors, are diversified (meaning that they operate in a number of different lines of business, which often encompass several industry groupings), we have previously shown that manufacturing firms' overall domestic-related R&D strategy can still be classified dichotomously as either innovative or imitative. This important finding is discussed in detail in the appendix to this chapter.

Firms adopting an innovative strategy are generally referred to as innovators, whereas those adopting an imitative strategy can be categorized by one of three behavioral labels: *fast imitator, midcycle imitator*, or *late entrant*. The dominant strategy chosen by a firm is not independent of the stage of development of the industry within which the technology-based product will be developed. These stages have already been discussed in Chapter 2, in relationship to figure 2–6, under the categories of the fluid stage, the transitional stage, and the specific stage of development.

An *innovator* adopting an innovative strategy is primarily concerned with capturing a large share of the market. Being first into the market with a new product or process establishes a temporary monopoly position. Innovators' ability to capitalize on this monopoly power depends, of course, on the design of the product or process. However, a potential user will not only consider the usefulness of the technology but also the potential of the technology for interfacing with other existing production processes, the reputation of the producer for maintenance and technical support, and the future availability of close substitutes at a lower cost. Performance, then, is the dominant consideration in this adoption decision. By definition, an innovator enters during the fluid stage of process development.

A *fast imitator* may be a well-established producer adept at obtaining a sizable market share through comparative advantages in product engineering, production, and marketing. Such a firm's strategy is to remain technologically abreast of current trends and wait until a rival imitator assesses the risk of entering the market with a new product or product design. By definition, the fast imitator can rapidly assess and replicate the innovator's product, and thus enter the market close on the heels of the innovator. The larger market share enjoyed by the fast imitator of the previously marketed, but now technologically outdated, product will confer a favorable reputation. Even though second into the market, the fast imitator will rapidly gain a strong market position, assuming that quality and all else remain constant. As with the innovator, the fast imitator enters the market during the fluid stage of process development. In other words, the fluid stage of development sees both innovative and imitative technology-based strategies being adopted and demonstrated.

A *midcycle imitator* enters the market during the transitional stage of the life cycle. Such a firm perceives an opportunity to imitate the dominant product technology's design, add improved process technology in order to sell it at a lower cost than its rivals, and combine low cost with superior marketing skills. As part of an imitative strategy, such a firm may find it most profitable to remain with its existing product rather than introduce a technologically-advanced substitute.

Late entrants enter in the static stage of the cycle. The market is well established at this time, the product is standardized in large part, and competition is based primarily on price. A late entrant may resemble the midcycle imitator, but with less reliance on process-related technical advances and more emphasis on technical service. Late entrants may attempt to reach a specialized segment of customers, who themselves are late adopters of the new product. They will purchase another firm's standardized product design, add specialized services, and then resell the product combined with the service package. Table 5–1 summarizes the relationship between these technology-based competitive strategies and the stage of process development originally illustrated in table 2–6.

Given the nature of formal cooperative research activity as constrained by the National Cooperative Research Act, it is likely that such activities will be undertaken in preparation for a firm to reenter the market during the fluid stage of the *next* production process life cycle. However, since the vast majority of research cooperation is informal in its nature, as evidenced by the information discussed in Chapter 4 and presented in table 4–5, it is quite possible that the results from cooperation can help position a firm to compete in *any* of the three stages just discussed. The specific strategic objective associated with the cooperative research undertakings discussed in the preceding chapter are analyzed here.

Interindustry Differences in Competitive Strategies

The information presented in the data tables in Chapter 4 indicates that there are sizable interindustry differences in the extent of cooperative research activity throughout the manufacturing sector. For example, as shown in table 4–8, in 1984 firms in instruments and related products (SIC 38) allocated over 12 percent of their internal R&D budget to cooperative

Table 5–1
Relationship between Technology-Based Competitive Strategies and Stages of Development

Competitive Strategy	Type of Firm	Stage when Implemented
Innovative	Innovator	Fluid
Imitative	Fast imitator	Fluid
Imitative	Midcycle imitator	Transitional
Imitative	Late entrant	Static

Source: Based on information in Albert N. Link and Gregory Tassey, *Strategies for Technology-Based Competition: Meeting the New Global Challenge* (Lexington, Mass.: Lexington Books, 1987), p. 23.

research endeavors, compared to just over a 2 percent allocation in the textile (SIC 22) and paper (SIC 26) industries.

These differences were examined in Chapter 4. Recall that the data presented in figure 4–1 suggest that interindustry differences in the percentage of R&D allocated to cooperative research are not, in general, related to the degree of foreign competition in the industries. It is related, though, among those industries that are active in cooperative research. Here, we examine interindustry differences in the motives for participating in cooperative research. The section that follows this one reconsiders this overview treatment by analyzing strategic motives at the firm level.

As part of our survey, each of the sixty-two cooperative research–active firms was asked to indicate the strategic objectives associated with its involvement in cooperative research. Specifically, the R&D vice-presidents were asked to distribute their total 1984 cooperative research projects, and the portion of their R&D budgets allocated to those projects, between the following three strategic objectives: *horizontal diversification* into new product lines, *vertical integration* (backward and forward), and *leapfrog competition* within existing product lines. These three strategy categories evolved from preliminary discussions with cooperative research–active R&D vice-presidents and from our pretests of the survey instrument.[3]

Table 5–2 summarizes information taken from Chapter 4 regarding the distribution of the 446 cooperative research projects undertaken by the subsample of sixty-two firms, presented here by two-digit SIC industry. Also in table 5–2 are the average percentages of R&D dollars allocated to cooperative research activities.

The analysis that follows considers all the fourteen industries shown in table 5–2 in which cooperative research projects were undertaken during 1984, regardless of the number of projects undertaken. Of course, an argument could be made that the validity of trying to allocate only a handful of projects undertaken by an even smaller handful of firms across three strategy groupings is questionable. We agree with such a proposition, but since our intent at this point is *only* descriptive, industries such as primary metals (SIC 33) and fabricated metals (SIC 34) are retained in the tables and in the analyses that follow.

In table 5–3 we report the distribution of all these 446 cooperative research projects across industries, by strategic objective. The strategy-related behavior at the industry level is quite diverse. Consider the industries more project-intensive in an absolute sense. In the paper and allied products industry (SIC 26), for example, 81 percent of the 43 projects undertaken were directed to horizontal diversification into new product lines, with the remaining 19 percent going toward leapfrog competition. In the paper industry no projects were aimed at vertical integration in 1984. Somewhat similar is the distribution across strategies in the chemicals in-

Table 5–2
Activities of Cooperative Research–Active Firms, by Two-Digit SIC Industry

SIC Code	Industry	n	Number of Projects	Percentage of R&D to CRVs
20	Food and kindred products	5	22	.058
21	Tobacco products	0	NA	NA
22	Textile mill products	1	6	.026
23	Apparel and other textile products	0	NA	NA
24	Lumber and wood products	0	NA	NA
25	Furniture and fixtures	0	NA	NA
26	Paper and allied products	2	43	.023
27	Printing and publishing	0	NA	NA
28	Chemicals and allied products	8	109	.073
29	Petroleum and coal products	7	65	.063
30	Rubber and miscellaneous plastic products	1	9	.055
31	Leather and leather products	0	NA	NA
32	Stone, clay, and glass products	2	21	.051
33	Primary metal industries	2	3	.040
34	Fabricated metal products	3	4	.062
35	Machinery, except electrical	10	61	.068
36	Electric and electronic equipment	10	75	.088
37	Transportation equipment	5	15	.081
38	Instruments and related products	4	8	.121
39	Miscellaneous manufacturing	2	5	.138
	Total	62	446	

dustry (SIC 28) and in the petroleum industry (SIC 29). In both of these project-intensive industries, the majority of the project activity was directed toward horizontal diversification with vertical integration being the activity least engaged in. In chemicals, 57 percent of the 109 cooperative research projects went toward horizontal diversification–related activities, and similarly for 62 percent of the 65 projects undertaken in the petroleum industry.

In comparison, leapfrog competition was the activity engaged in most intensely, in a project sense, in the stone, clay, and glass industry (SIC 32); in the electric and electronic equipment industry (SIC 36); and in the transportation equipment industry (SIC 37). In stone, clay, and glass, 62 percent of the 21 cooperative research projects were aimed toward a leapfrog competitive strategy. The corresponding percentage in the electronic

Table 5–3
Distribution of Cooperative Research Projects by Strategic Objective

SIC Code	Industry	n	HDPCT#	VIPCT#	LFCPCT#
20	Food and kindred products	22	.54	.10	.36
21	Tobacco products	0	NA	NA	NA
22	Textile mill products	6	.67	0	.33
23	Apparel and other textile products	0	NA	NA	NA
24	Lumber and wood products	0	NA	NA	NA
25	Furniture and fixtures	0	NA	NA	NA
26	Paper and allied products	43	.81	0	.19
27	Printing and publishing	0	NA	NA	NA
28	Chemicals and allied products	109	.57	.19	.24
29	Petroleum and coal products	65	.62	.12	.26
30	Rubber and miscellaneous plastic products	9	.56	0	.44
31	Leather and leather products	0	NA	NA	NA
32	Stone, clay, and glass products	21	.19	.19	.62
33	Primary metal industries	3	.33	.33	.34
34	Fabricated metal products	4	.25	.50	.25
35	Machinery, except electrical	61	.21	.43	.36
36	Electric and electronic equipment	75	.34	.11	.55
37	Transportation equipment	15	.13	.20	.67
38	Instruments and related products	8	.38	.12	.50
39	Miscellaneous manufacturing	5	.80	0	.20
	Total	446			

Note: HDPCT#: percentage of cooperative research projects whose strategic objective is horizontal diversification into new product lines.

VIPCT#: percentage of cooperative research projects whose strategic objective is vertical integration (backward or forward).

LFCPCT#: percentage of cooperative research projects whose strategic objective is leapfrog competition within existing product lines.

HDPCT# + VIPCT# + LFCPCT# = 1.0.

equipment industry is 55, and it is 67 in the transportation equipment industry.

In our opinion, two dominant patterns of project activity emerge from table 5–3. One, we can conclude from this survey information that cooperative research is not undertaken for a single strategic reason. The strategic motives underlying cooperation are varied. Two, if there is a dominant strategy within an industry it generally is either horizontal diversification into new product lines or leapfrog competition. Only in the fabricated metal products industry is vertical integration dominant.

In table 5–4, cooperative research spending (as opposed to project activity) by strategic objective is illustrated on an industry-by-industry basis. The percentages in the last three columns of the table are the percentages of the cooperative R&D budget allocated to each of the three predefined strategic groupings. With reference to the more project-intensive industries noted in the previous paragraph, a similar allocation pattern exists but not an exact one. In the paper and allied products industry (SIC 26), horizontal diversification is the dominant strategy, as evidenced both by the percentage of projects in that category (81 percent in table 5–3) and by the reported 93 percent of cooperative R&D so spent. In chemicals and allied products (SIC 28), whereas 57 percent of the cooperative projects were aimed toward horizontal diversification, only 24 percent were aimed

Table 5–4
Distribution of Cooperative Research Spending by Strategic Objective

SIC Code	Industry	HDPCT$	VIPCT$	LFCPCT$
20	Food and kindred products	.55	.19	.26
21	Tobacco products	NA	NA	NA
22	Textile mill products	.88	0	.12
23	Apparel and other textile products	NA	NA	NA
24	Lumber and wood products	NA	NA	NA
25	Furniture and fixtures	NA	NA	NA
26	Paper and allied products	.93	0	.07
27	Printing and publishing	NA	NA	NA
28	Chemicals and allied products	.45	.05	.50
29	Petroleum and coal products	.54	.30	.16
30	Rubber and miscellaneous plastic products	.55	0	.45
31	Leather and leather products	NA	NA	NA
32	Stone, clay, and glass products	.41	.09	.50
33	Primary metal industries	.63	.07	.30
34	Fabricated metal products	.23	.58	.19
35	Machinery, except electrical	.48	.24	.28
36	Electric and electronic equipment	.31	.37	.32
37	Transportation equipment	.22	.57	.21
38	Instruments and related products	.33	.20	.47
39	Miscellaneous manufacturing	.90	0	.10

Note: *HDPCT$:* percentage of cooperative R&D allocated to research activity whose strategic objective is horizontal diversification into new product lines.

        VIPCT$: percentage of cooperative R&D allocated to research activity whose strategic objective is vertical integration (backward or forward).

        LFCPCT$: percentage of cooperative R&D allocated to research activity whose strategic objective is leapfrog competition within existing product lines.

        HDPCT$ + VIPCT$ + LFCPCT$ = 1.0.

at leapfrog competition. In fact, in chemicals the dollar allocations shown in table 5–4 are approximately equal between the two categories: 45 percent to horizontal diversification and 50 percent to leapfrog competition. In the petroleum and coal products industry (SIC 29), the contrast between project allocations and R&D allocations is less dramatic. In that industry, horizontal diversification dominates, but the project allocation and dollar allocation between vertical integration and leapfrog competition are reversed in tables 5–3 and 5–4. By projects, the rank of strategic motives in the petroleum industry (from most active to least active) is horizontal diversification, leapfrog competition, then vertical integration. By R&D spending, the rank in that industry is horizontal diversification, vertical integration, then leapfrog competition.

In stone, clay, and glass (SIC 32), the majority of projects undertaken were aimed at leapfrog competition by nearly a three-to-one margin (62 percent compared to 19 percent). But in terms of dollars actually spent, the allocation is more balanced between horizontal diversification and leapfrog competition (41 percent compared to 50 percent, respectfully), with only 9 percent of the budget going to vertical integration.

In machinery (SIC 35), vertical integration appears to be the dominant strategy, when evaluated on a project basis. Using R&D spending, horizontal diversification is clearly the dominant strategic objective.

In the electric and electronic equipment industry (SIC 36), and in the transportation equipment industry (SIC 37), the allocations of projects reported in table 5–3 are skewed toward leapfrog competition, 55 percent and 67 percent, respectively. But, in table 5–4 the corresponding budget allocations are more even across the three categories: 31 to 37 to 32 percent in electronic equipment and 22 to 57 to 21 percent in transportation. More specifically, the budget allocations are definitely not skewed toward leapfrog competition.

Table 5–5 shows, for the fourteen two-digit industries that are active in cooperative research, the correlation coefficients between the percentage of cooperative research projects aimed at a particular strategy with the percentage of cooperative R&D allocated toward the corresponding strategy. Although differences do exist, over all fourteen industries there is a positive relationship between these allocation patterns. The strongest correlation is with respect to horizontal diversification: the correlation coefficient is 0.83 and it is highly significant. The weakest correlation is with respect to leapfrog competition.

As we noted in Chapter 4, we believe that the percentages reflecting R&D budget allocations are a more meaningful statistic when compared across industry (and later across firms) than are the project percentages. In figure 4–1, we illustrated graphically the relationship between the percentage of R&D allocated to cooperation and the corresponding degree of

Table 5–5
Correlation between Percentage of Cooperative Research Projects and Percentage of Cooperative R&D Budget Allocated to Alternative Strategic Objectives (n = 14)

	HDPCT#	VIPCT#	LFCPCT#
HDPCT$:	0.83***	—	—
VIPCT$:	—	0.57**	—
LFCPCT$:	—	—	0.49*

Note: See notes in tables 5–3 and 5–4 for definitions of the variables.

  *Significant at the .10 level.
 **Significant at the .05 level.
***Significant at the .01 level.

foreign competition in each industry. A similar exercise is illustrated in figure 5–1.

Figure 5–1 shows diagrams of the percentage of cooperative R&D allocated to each of the three strategy groups, as a function of foreign competition in the same industry. For any category, one would be hard pressed to conclude that foreign competition is systematically related in interindustry differences in competitive strategies. In our opinion, the three scatter diagrams in figure 5–1 appear to reveal a random pattern. This issue is reexamined in the next section in terms of the influence of foreign competition on interfirm differences in competitive strategies.

Interfirm Differences in Competitive Strategies

The Analytical Framework

To investigate interfirm differences in competitive strategies, as defined earlier, we focus on the same set of explanatory variables that was discussed in Chapter 4: foreign competition, profits, and market power. The analytical results presented in Chapter 4, tables 4–10 and 4–12, indicate clearly that foreign competition influences a firm's decision to engage in cooperative research. Specifically, we showed in Chapter 4 that increases in foreign competition directly influence a firm's decision to engage in cooperation. The influence of foreign competition is greater on the initial decision to undertake cooperative research than on the incremental decision to spend relatively more or less on that activity.

It is an empirical issue as to how foreign competition influences the strategic choices associated with cooperation, once the decision to cooper-

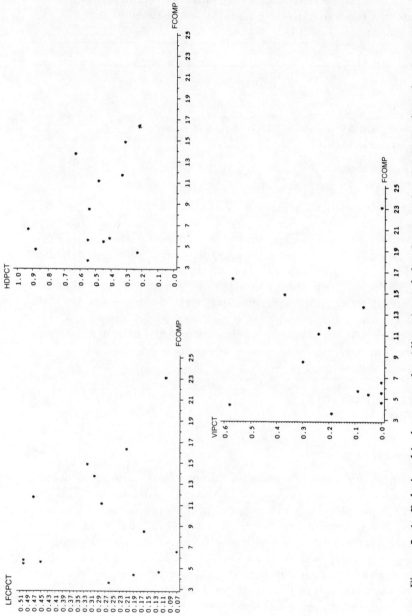

Figure 5–1. Relationship between the Allocation of the Cooperative R&D Budget, by Strategic Objective, and the Extent of Foreign Competition ($n = 14$)

Note: *FCOMP* represents the import share associated with each industry, as defined in the text.

ate is made. Our only hypothesis on this matter is that increases in foreign competition are unlikely to influence the extent to which leapfrog competition is undertaken. That strategy, in our opinion, is practiced primarily in response to domestic rivalry where market niches are better understood.

Regarding interfirm differences in the percentage of R&D allocated to cooperative research, we did not posit any definite directional influence with respect to profits. And, the empirical results presented in table 4–10 did not shed any statistical light on that issue.

Regarding the influence of profits on the use of cooperative research to pursue alternative competitive strategies, the conceptual issue is equally unclear. Firms adopt competitive strategies, in general, in pursuit of higher profits. It may be the case that waning profits provide an incentive for firms to undertake a strategy that has a near-term payoff. From our discussions with corporate officers involved in the management of cooperative research projects, successful leapfrog competition within existing product lines parallels the near-term payoff objective more than does horizontal diversification or vertical integration. Based on this knowledge, we hypothesize that there will be an inverse relationship between profits and the intensity to which a cooperative research–active firm pursues a leapfrog competitive strategy. We offer no hypothesis regarding the influence of profits on horizontal diversification or vertical integration.

As with profits, the evidence related to the influence of market power on cooperative research activity is mixed, as discussed in Chapter 4. Here, we offer no hypotheses about the influence of industry concentration on strategy choices, but we do hypothesize about the relationship between market share and strategy choice.

We posit that, as market share increases, the marginal benefits associated with leapfrog competition decrease. Simply, as a firm's market share increases, the portion of the market claimed by its competitors decreases, by definition. Viewing antitrust concerns as somewhat of a deterrent and knowing that there are diminishing returns to R&D endeavors, the costs associated with gaining an increment of the market likely outweigh the financial benefits of that additional share. Therefore, we hypothesize an inverse relationship between market share and the extent to which a firm engages in leapfrog competition. We offer no hypothesis about the influence of market share on horizontal diversification or vertical integration.

The Statistical Analysis

The model used to investigate the influence of these factors on the allocation of cooperative R&D between strategic objectives is

$$\left.\begin{array}{l} HDPCT\$ \\ VIPCT\$ \\ LFCPCT\$ \end{array}\right\} = f(FCOMP,\ PROFIT,\ WCR,\ WMS)$$

As noted in table 5–4, *HDPCT$* is the percentage of the firm's cooperative R&D budget allocated to research activity whose strategic objective is horizontal diversification into new product lines; *VIPCT$* is the percentage of the firm's cooperative R&D budget allocated to research activity whose strategic objective is vertical integration (backward or forward); and *LFCPCT$* is the percentage of the firm's cooperative R&D budget allocated to research activity whose strategic objective is leapfrog competition within existing product lines. For each of the sixty-two firms in this subsample, the sum of these three percentages equals unity, by definition.

The independent variables have previously been defined in Chapter 4. *FCOMP* represents the extent of foreign competition faced by the firm, *PROFIT* is the firm's profit-to-sales ratio, *WCR* represents the weighted four-digit SIC industry concentration ratio associated with each firm's major line of business, and *WMS* represents the firm's weighted market share.

Since the dependent variables in this specification sum to unity and since each of the three relationships contains the same independent variables, ordinary least-squares is the appropriate estimating technique. The following equations were estimated using least-squares analysis:

$$HDPCT\$ = \alpha_0 + \alpha_1 FCOMP + \alpha_2 PROFIT + \alpha_3 WCR + \alpha_4 WMS + \alpha_5 D_i + \epsilon_1 \quad (5.1)$$

$$VIPCT\$ = \beta_0 + \beta_1 FCOMP + \beta_2 PROFIT + \beta_3 WCR + \beta_4 WMS + \beta_5 D_i + \epsilon_2 \quad (5.2)$$

$$LFCPCT\$ = \gamma_0 + \gamma_1 FCOMP + \gamma_2 PROFIT + \gamma_3 WCR + \gamma_4 WMS + \gamma_5 D_i + \epsilon_3 \quad (5.3)$$

where D_i are binary variables representing the two-digit SIC industry corresponding to each firm.[4] As previously stated, the dependent variables sum to unity: $HDPCT\$ + VIPCT\$ + LFCPCT\$ = 1.0$. By virtue of this constraint, it follows that the error terms, ϵ_i, are not independent, so the regression intercept terms sum to unity and the other regression coefficients sum to zero, across equations:

$$\alpha_0 + \beta_0 + \gamma_0 = 1.0$$

$$\alpha_1 + \beta_1 + \gamma_1 = 0.0$$

$$\alpha_2 + \beta_2 + \gamma_2 = 0.0$$

$$\alpha_3 + \beta_3 + \gamma_3 = 0.0$$

$$\alpha_4 + \beta_4 + \gamma_4 = 0.0$$

$$\alpha_5 + \beta_5 + \gamma_5 = 0.0$$

for each D_i.

The regression results from estimating equations (5.1) through (5.3) indicate that, as a group, the industry variables are not significant. Hence, they were deleted from further consideration. The least-squares results from these three equations, absent the variables D_i, are reported in table 5–6.

Perhaps the single most important thing to observe from the table is that a significant amount of the interfirm variation in the choice of strategic objectives is left *unexplained*. Certainly, a number of complicated intraorganizational aspects of strategy determination are not captured by our more aggregated independent variables. Also, there probably exists some interfirm differences in the interpretation of the three strategy categories that were used to constrain the data. (Regarding this latter point, efforts were made through pretesting the survey instrument to standardize our categories using language that *seemed* to correspond to the vocabulary of the respondents, but imprecisions certainly remain.) Even with these caveats, the estimated results are extremely interesting, and they do provide some useful insights into the scope of cooperative R&D activity.

As shown in Chapter 4, firms engage in cooperative research as a strategic response to foreign competition. The results in table 5–6 suggest that such cooperative research is aimed at horizontal diversification, although we did not hypothesize it. The estimated coefficient on *FCOMP* is positive and highly significant (for that dependent variable). Although not predicted, the significance of *FCOMP* in the leapfrog competition equation reinforces our intuition that U.S. firms do not yet view R&D as an offen-

Table 5–6
Least-Squares Regression Results for Equations (5.1)–(5.3) (*t*- statistics reported in parentheses: *n* = 62)

Independent Variable	Dependent	Variable	
	HDPCT$	VIPCT$	LFCPCT$
FCOMP	0.011	−0.001	−0.010
	(2.70)**	(−0.31)	(−2.51)**
PROFIT	−0.756	−0.541	1.297
	(−0.57)	(−0.48)	(1.00)
WCR	0.028	0.177	−0.205
	(0.13)	(0.98)	(−0.98)
WMS	−1.055	1.546	−0.491
	(−2.60)**	(4.52)**	(−1.99)*
Constant	0.397	0.025	0.578
	(3.28)**	(0.24)	(4.87)**
R^2	0.19	0.35	0.18
F- level	3.35*	7.55**	3.18*

*Significant at the .05 level.
**Significant at the .01 level.

sive weapon to use within world markets (although they view it that way within domestic markets, as discussed in the appendix to this chapter). Firm profits and the concentration of the industry in which the firm participates are not significant factors in explaining the strategic nature of their cooperative research. None of the corresponding regression coefficients on *PROFIT* or *WCR* approach conventional levels of significance.

Across these strategy categories, the dominant explanatory variable is the firm's market share. As we hypothesized, increases in market share redirect firms' strategic objectives away from leapfrog competition and away from horizontal diversification, although we did not posit that relationship, toward vertical integration. Perhaps, this reflects the fact that once market dominance is achieved, continued competition occurs in terms of cost reduction and, perhaps, price variation.

Concluding Statement

If nothing else, this chapter emphasizes the heterogeneity of the use of R&D expenditures among manufacturing firms. It has long been known that a number of activities are commonly grouped under the rubric of R&D spending. The National Science Foundation reporting categories, which were formalized in the 1950s, created a mind set among many academicians and policy makers that all R&D activity could easily be categorized under the trichotomy of basic research, applied research, and development. However, case studies have shown that other categorical labels are more closely aligned with the way R&D is actually used.

The information presented in this chapter takes us one step closer to understanding this reality. To our knowledge, this chapter represents the first systematic investigation, besides the results presented in the appendix to this chapter, into the strategic aspects associated with R&D spending patterns. Albeit that our focus is on cooperative research, our findings are sufficiently strong to encourage further investigations into this general topic.

What we have shown is that R&D-related strategies vary across firms, and they vary systematically in regard to the competitive environment of the firm. (They also show that our understanding of the institutional nature of cooperative research strategies is incomplete, as evidenced by our inability to hypothesize directional influences more completely.) The dominating influences in our regression analyses are the foreign competition variable and the market share variable, both of which obviously capture some aspect of a firm's competitive environment. This environment, as theory has long predicted, has a direct impact on the nature of a firm's activities, cooperative R&D in particular. For example, a firm without any significant degree of market power within an industry that faces intense foreign competition (that is, a firm with a low market share in an industry with a high import share) will respond, on average, by undertaking cooperative R&D and directing those activities toward horizontal diversification.

Not only do such insights help us better to understand the nature of technology-based competition but also may be useful to policy makers as they continue to look toward initiatives to improve the innovative posture of U.S. industries and their associated productivity growth.

Appendix 5A: Innovation versus Imitation—Alternative R&D Strategies

Few topics in the literature on the economics of technology—or the broader industrial organization literature for that matter—have received as much attention as the relationship between market power, firm size, and innovative activity. Investigators have addressed two important and related issues: Is it the possession of, or rather the quest for, market power that stimulates innovation? Is firm size, apart from market power, related to the level of innovative activity?

Much of the empirical literature surrounding these two questions has focused on *levels* of R&D spending as a proxy for innovative activity. As we showed in Chapter 4, and to a greater extent in the body of Chapter 5, R&D spending encompasses myriad activities. Firms employ different R&D strategies, broadly delineated as innovative or imitative. R&D spending is important for the success of *either* strategy; therefore, interfirm differences in R&D spending per se are questionable indicators of firms' differences in innovativeness.[5]

Based on telephone interviews in 1980 with the R&D vice-presidents from seventy-six of the dominant R&D-active corporations in the U.S. manufacturing sector, we were able to characterize each firm's *overall* R&D strategy as innovative or imitative. Surprisingly, no R&D vice-president had difficulty in characterizing the firm's overall R&D program dichotomously, even in the more highly diversified firms.

To investigate interfirm differences in R&D strategy, we regressed this dichotomous variable against each firm's size (measured as the logarithm of its 1980 sales in millions of dollars), *SIZE*; its weighted market share, *WMS*; and the weighted four-firm concentration ratio corresponding to each firm's major line of business, *WCR*. The logit coefficient on *SIZE* is positive and highly significant; that on *WMS* is also positive and significant; but the logit coefficient on *WCR* is negative and insignificant (see table 5–7).

Table 5–7

Estimated Logit Results Explaining the Innovative versus Imitative Strategy Choice (asymptotic t- statistics in parentheses: $n = 76$)

Independent Variable	Coefficient
SIZE	1.875
	(3.69)**
WMS	0.193
	(2.43)*
WCR	−0.043
	(−1.41)
−2 × log likelihood ratio	43.19

*Significant at the .05 level.
**Significant at the .01 level.

Although these results are not directly comparable with the regression results presented in the body of Chapter 5, they emphasize two important things: one, market share is an important factor in a firm's choice of an R&D strategy; and two, industry concentration is not (despite the continuing quest to prove it so in the academic literature).

6
Cooperative Research and the Production of Knowledge

A frequently asked question is, What is the output from R&D activity? Unfortunately, as is often the case, it is easier to ask this question than to answer it. One answer frequently given is that *knowledge* is the output from the R&D process. This is, in fact, true, but it does not provide much comfort to those interested in quantifying the R&D process in an input-to-output framework. Some have looked at patents as a solution, with mixed success.

We are interested in exploring here the answer to a related question; What is the output from cooperative research activity? We must emphasize (perhaps in somewhat of a defensive vein) that this chapter is indeed *exploratory* in nature. Still, we believe that the information that we have been able to gather is useful in that it provides guideposts for managers already engaged in cooperative activities as well as for scholars who will conduct the research that follows.

Theoretical Consequences of Cooperative Research

Perhaps, the first place to start to answer the question about the output that results from cooperative research is with a conceptual model of the cooperative research process. Although this book is descriptive in nature, at this point we call upon theory to verify the output measures that are described later. In this opening section, we demonstrate that one output from cooperation is additional R&D, and that this additional R&D is oriented toward basic research–related activities.[1]

The maintained assumption of this model is that R&D is an investment into the production of technical knowledge, and that technical knowledge has the characteristics of a public good (an important point that was emphasized in Chapter 3). This assumption is motivated on the belief that technical knowledge is not fully appropriated by the firm conducting the R&D, and hence it will, over time, diffuse throughout the industry and the economy. Technical knowledge can either diffuse as information per se or as information embodied in new vintages of capital.

In what follows we treat R&D as a homogeneous input into the production of knowledge when, in fact, we know that the activities broadly grouped under that rubric are heterogeneous in scope. We make this assumption for simplicity and feel that the implications of the model are not greatly affected by it.

Assume that an industry is composed of two firms: Firm A and Firm B. Both firms invest independently in basic research activity. The technical knowledge obtained from the basic research endeavors is assumed to have characteristics of a public good. With reference to figure 6–1, Firm A is

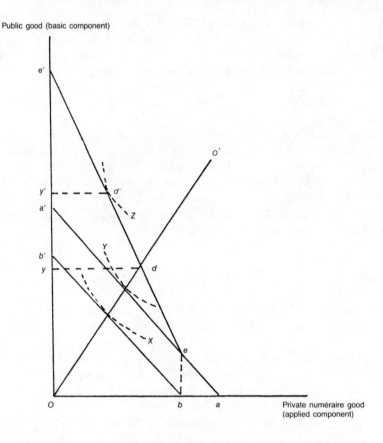

Figure 6–1. A Public Good Model of R&D Spending

Source: Adapted from Barry Bozeman, Albert N. Link, and Asghar Zardkoohi, "An Economic Analysis of R&D Joint Ventures," *Managerial and Decision Economics* (August 1986): p 264.

assumed to have an initial endowment of resources (a numéraire good) denoted by Oa on the horizontal axis, and Firm B is assumed to have an initial endowment of the numéraire good denoted by Ob. The initial endowment in each case can be thought of as the budgeted R&D that can either be allocated to the applied component of R&D (a private good), the basic component (a public good), or any linear combination of the two. The specific transformation curves between the two components are denoted by aa' and bb' for Firms A and B, respectively. The slope of these transformation curves represents the marginal cost of producing a unit of technical knowledge in terms of the applied component. The X, Y, and Z curves can be thought of as the isoprofit curves. The ray OO' represents the locus of optimal investment choices for the two firms, acting independently.

Since the objective of our graphical exercise is to compare the provision of the public good when investments are made both independently and through cooperation, we must determine each firm's investment choice under the two alternatives. If each firm invests its entire endowment of the numéraire good on the public good, the total amount provided will be Oe' ($Oe' = Oa' + Ob'$) and each firm, assuming perfect diffusion, will have an allocation denoted by point e'. But, of course, point e' is away from the locus of optimal investment choices. Each firm maximizes profits, given its transformation curve, by attempting to reach an allocation on the optimal locus, OO'. Since each firm independently moves to the optimal investment locus, OO' and since both firms eventually must use identical amounts of the public good (by definition of a public good), it necessarily follows that both firms must simultaneously reach an identical and unique allocation on OO'. To find this unique allocation, we must first determine the locus of all possible allocations that both firms can reach simultaneously. The intersection of this latter locus and OO' determines such a unique point (which both Firm A and Firm B obtain simultaneously). Note that the unique, or identical, allocation implies that both firms end up having identical bundles of the two goods, regardless of their initial endowments of the numéraire good.

One allocation that both firms can obtain simultaneously is e'. If Firm A invests Oa' and Firm B invests Ob' in the public good, then Oe' will be the total amount produced and e' will be the allocation facing both firms. There are, of course, an infinite number of such allocations that both firms can obtain simultaneously. These can be found by taking the feasible allocations on the horizontal axis that both firms can reach, and then finding the corresponding amounts of the public good obtained by the firms. Since Firm B cannot obtain endowments exceeding Ob, the feasible points that can be attained by the firms must be limited to Ob. Take, for example, point b. Firm B spends zero amount on the public good whereas Firm A spends *ba* amount and provides *be*. Both firms reach the *e* allocation simultaneously, having identical amounts of both goods. Connecting *e* to *e'*, we find all of the allocations that can be achieved by both firms simultaneously. The intersection between *ee'* and *OO'*, point *d*, determines the equilibrium allocations obtained by both firms, given independent adjustments. The allocation at *d* is unique in that both firms reach that allocation simultaneously. It shows that the firms end up receiving identical amounts of the public good as well as the private good, although the initial endowments were different. The logic is that both firms attempt to find an allocation on the *OO'* curve; furthermore, they receive the same amount of the public good. Being on *OO'* and receiving the same amount of the public good implies that the firms will reach an identical allocation simultaneously, identified as *d* in figure 6–1. The allocation at *d* is not, of course, an economically efficient allocation since the slope of *ee'* is different from that of *aa'* or *bb'*. Both Firms A and B can be made better off by moving to the allocation at *d'*. This point can be reached only through cooperation in R&D. If cooperation were not practiced, the free rider problem would inhibit such a move. Cooperation will increase the amount of technical knowledge from *Oy* to *Oy'*.

Our theoretical conclusion that cooperation increases R&D and the total amount of technical knowledge so generated is not dependent on the fact that the model in figure 6–1 is based on only two firms. We extend that model in figure 6–2 to include three firms of sizes *Oa*, *Ob*, and *Oc*. There, line *dd'* represents the locus of all points that Firms A and B can reach at the same time, assuming that Firm C produced no public good. Rays from the origin intersecting line *ee'*, will obtain full allocation equalization across the three firms, with each firm having equal amounts of the public good and, of course, the private good. However, rays intersecting line *de* will result in allocation equalization for Firms A and B, with Firm C receiving identical amounts of the public good but only *Oc* of the private good. In a multifirm world with identical trade-off relationships between private and public goods, independent public good investments will result in final allocation equalization among these firms that provide the public good.

Our model predicts clearly that the total level of R&D spending between the two firms (within the same industry) will increase as a result of their cooperative research. We posit that firms engaging in cooperative research have their own incentives for directing their investment spending toward basic research. Since basic research has more public good characteristics than applied research or development, firms would not be able to appropriate fully the resulting knowledge if the research were conducted privately. Hence, they may be more willing to share in those basic costs.

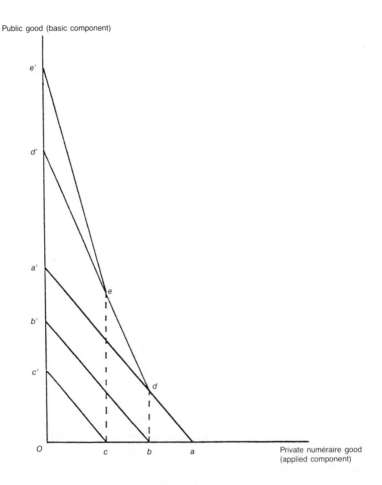

Figure 6–2. An Extension of the Graphic Model in Figure 6–1

Source: Adapted from Barry Bozeman, Albert N. Link, and Asghar Zardkoohi, "An Economic Analysis of R&D Joint Ventures," *Managerial and Decision Economics* (August 1986): p 265.

We know that there are financial economies of scale associated with R&D as a whole, and thus it may be safe to conclude that, owing to the greater uncertainty of basic undertakings, the financial economies are even greater. Therefore, cost sharing via cooperation may be especially attractive for basic endeavors, given the self interest constraints firms often face for R&D.

Quantifying the Output from
Cooperative Research

In 1987, we followed up our 1986 survey with a second survey to all of the R&D vice presidents (or designates) who participated in the first study. All sixty-two cooperative research–active firms were contacted. Our intent was to obtain some information about the output that had resulted from their 1984 cooperative research activities. Specifically, we asked the following questions: (1) approximately, how many new products have resulted, to date, from the 1984 cooperative research ventures? (2) approximately, how many new production processes have resulted, to date, from the 1984 cooperative research ventures? (3) approximately, how many new patents have been applied for, to date, as a result of the 1984 cooperative research ventures? and, (4) approximately, how many new patents have been obtained, to date, as a result of the 1984 cooperative research ventures? The instructions were clear that the respondents should include in their answers only those activities that would *not* have been undertaken without cooperation. Our goal was to ascertain information on the output that could be produced only as a result of cooperation. This point was reemphasized in telephone interviews with each respondent to recheck the accuracy of the reported information and to assure cross-firm consistency in the responses. In order to ensure additional consistency, each firm's earlier responses were included in the survey and the same individual was urged to respond to the new instrument as responded to the initial instrument.

After a second mailing, we obtained information from forty-eight of the sixty-two firms. Fortunately, thirty-eight of these firms were within the original group of forty firms from the following five industries: food and kindred products (SIC 20), chemicals and allied products (SIC 28), petroleum and coal products (SIC 29), machinery, except electrical (SIC 35), and electric and electronic equipment (SIC 36). We report in table 6–1 the distribution of these thirty-eight firms across these five two-digit industry groupings. We also report in that table the number of cooperative research projects undertaken in 1984 and the percentage of internal R&D allocated to cooperative research activities, averaged across firms within each industry, based on information reported earlier in Chapter 4.

Table 6–2 lists the responses to the four survey questions reproduced earlier, averaged across firms in each industry. For example, in the food industry, the average number of new products developed per firm as a result of the 1984 cooperative research ventures is 3.8. On average, each firm in that industry also developed 0.2 new production processes based on their earlier cooperative research. None of the cooperative activity undertaken by these food industry firms led to patent applications or patents received.

Table 6–1
Subsample of Cooperative Research–Active Firms Providing Output Information for 1987

SIC Code	Industry	n	Number CRV Projects	% R&D to CRVs
20	Food and kindred products	5	22	.058
28	Chemicals and allied products	8	109	.073
29	Petroleum and coal products	7	65	.063
35	Machinery, except electrical	9	57*	.064*
36	Electric and electronic equipment	9	59*	.086*
	Total	38	312	

*These industries are not fully represented, thus the data reported are different from the data shown in tables 4–5 and 4–8 and elsewhere.

The reported output in the chemicals industry is more patent-intensive than in the food industry. On average, each of the eight firms in that industry applied for 6.5 patents as a result of their earlier cooperative endeavors. The lag time between application and receipt of a patent is very long in the chemicals industry. This institutional fact probably explains why no patents had yet been received by these firms. It also appears to be the case in chemicals that cooperative research led to more process-related output than product-related output: 3.4 compared to 1.25, per firm.

Cooperation among the petroleum firms also seems to have been directed toward patentable activity, on average 3.1 applications per firm; and to the development of new products, on average 2.7 new products per firm. No patents were received by firms in that industry, perhaps also reflecting a characteristically long lag time.

The machinery industry is interesting because little output is reported to have resulted from the earlier cooperative research undertakings of the

Table 6–2
Average Output from Cooperative Research Projects, by Selected Industry

Output Category	Food	Chemicals	Petroleum	Machinery	Electronic Equipment
New products	3.8	1.25	2.7	0.3	3.7
New processes	0.2	3.4	0.9	1.8	4.2
Patent applications	0.0	6.5	3.1	0.1	0.6
Patents received	0.0	0.0	0.0	0.1	0.0

nine firms represented. What did result seems to be process-related in its use.

Finally, the nine firms in the electronic equipment industry are active in the production of both new products and new processes but far less active in patentable applications than firms in the chemicals or petroleum industries. These electronic equipment firms' earlier cooperative research led to, on average, 3.7 new products per firm and 4.2 new production processes per firm.

Although subjective in nature, the information reported in table 6–2 is still interesting. One conclusion we can draw from this exercise is that firms are conscious of their cooperative relationships and aware that only through cooperation can certain activities be completed. In other words, in the minds of these firms' R&D vice presidents, the outputs *directly* attributable to their earlier cooperative efforts are distinct and noticeable.

We asked one additional question of the R&D vice presidents of these thirty-eight firms. We were interested in their perception about the extent to which their strategic motives for undertaking cooperative research were being realized three years later. In our instrument we used several open-ended questions to probe at this important issue. From studying these often lengthy responses and follow-up discussions both by telephone and in person (see Chapter 7), we arrived at the following conclusions:

• Cooperative research is an efficient mechanism for horizontal diversification. It does, however, bring about some personnel and administrative problems (discussed in Chapter 7) that are not encountered in the more traditional R&D settings. The technical knowledge needed to enter new markets more *quickly* is produced at what generally is viewed as a lower cost compared to a solo investigation. However, only a handful of respondents could document any formal mechanism for evaluating this claim.

• In general, cooperative strategies undertaken to achieve more vertical integration were not perceived to be successful. The consensus was that sufficient time had elapsed to see results from these undertakings, but few could be identified. With the exception of two very large, research-intensive firms, the respondents said that their firms anticipated looking back toward merger activity as a more direct and predictable way to integrate vertically.

• The recorded responses to our survey questions clearly indicated that cooperation in research does assist in achieving leapfrog advantages, especially among those firms with the relatively lower share of the targeted line of business.

Productivity Growth Implications of Cooperative Research

What We Know about Productivity Growth

Productivity growth[2] is vital to economic well-being because it enhances standards of living and the quality of life. It improves production efficiency, which in turn enhances the competitive, financial, and military position of a nation within the international community. It increases income, which potentially can be reallocated toward improving conditions of social concern such as environmental pollution or poverty and thereby also enhancing quality of life. Productivity advances ameliorate inflationary pressures and thus help establish economic stability. And, productivity growth stimulates market competition within an economy and among economies, thus improving resource allocation in general.

One phenomenon responsible for productivity growth is technological change or technical progress. Technological change brings about production efficiencies, which in turn lead to productivity growth. To understand the concept of productivity growth better, it is imperative also to understand the nature of technological change and the link between the two concepts.

The importance of technical progress and economic growth has long been known to students of economics. Contemporary interest in the topic was spurred as a result of several empirical studies during the 1950s, which concluded that technological change was the most important single factor associated with aggregate economic growth. Partly as a result of these studies, a body of academic literature began to grow. Its focus was on the technology-to-productivity growth relationship, the economics of growth itself, and the microeconomic foundations of technological change. In the 1970s, the apparent retardation of productivity growth in most industrialized nations and in their firms revived the interest of scholars, policy makers, and corporate leaders in these topics.

There is no single, generally accepted way to measure productivity or productivity growth at either the aggregate level or at the level of one particular firm (or organization within a firm). The more common measures begin with a conceptual representation of an input-to-output transformation process usually referred to as a *production function*. A production function is not viewed by all as a valid point of departure; nevertheless, given this conceptualization, productivity may be thought of as the degree of efficiency exhibited in the process of turning inputs into output.

Specifically, *total factor productivity* describes the ratio of output to the combination of all inputs used. *Partial factor productivity* measures a ratio of output to the amount of one single input, usually labor. If output, Q, and a vector of n inputs $(x_1, x_2, \ldots, x_n)$, denoted by X, are related as

$$Q = A(t)f(X) \tag{6.1}$$

where $A(t)$ is a time-related shift factor, then total factor productivity, *TFP*, can be approximated as

$$TFP = A(t) = Q/f(X) = Q/\Sigma w_i x_i \tag{6.2}$$

where the w_is are the individual input weights, assumed to be within the positive unit interval. Using this same notation, partial factor productivity can be written as Q/x_i.

Table 6–3 reports the average annual percentage rates of change between 1948 and 1986 for total factor productivity and labor productivity for the U.S. business economy, for the manufacturing sector, and for the twenty two-digit industries within the manufacturing sector. The two indices differ, as they should. Labor productivity measures are larger than total factor productivity measures because capital productivity is accounted for only in the latter.

As suggested earlier, the episode that renewed the interest of many in the concept of productivity growth and in the factors that are associated with changes in productivity growth was its pronounced decline in the mid-1960s and again in the early- 1970s. For example, labor productivity in the private business sector fell from 3.3 percent per year between 1948 and 1965, to 2.3 percent between 1965 and 1973, to 1.2 percent between 1973 and 1978. Some modest recovery has been made during the 1980s. Total factor productivity growth rates exhibit a similar trend beginning in the mid-1960s, with the decline accelerating after about 1973. In fact, total factor productivity growth in the 1973–1978 period was the lowest since, at least, World War II.

Productivity growth is a fundamental contributor to overall economic well-being. Because of this, the persistent slowdown in productivity growth since the mid-1960s that plagued many economies and their industrial sectors, *and* the more pervasive slowdown since 1973, has caused considerable concern. Why did productivity growth slow? Is the slow recovery of the 1980s real? Can the recovery be sustained?

The following factors are believed to be associated with these two slowdowns. Although the accompanying discussion is focused, in large part, at an aggregate level, the lessons learned from such inquiries is directly useful to management in several ways. First, it provides useful knowledge for managers on how better to interpret their economic environment, this

Table 6–3
Average Annual Productivity Growth Rates, by Sector and Industry, 1948–1986

Sector or Industry	Total Factor Productivity	Labor Productivity
U.S. business economy	1.7	2.2
Manufacturing sector	2.1	2.7
Food and kindred products	2.5	3.0
Tobacco products	0.4	2.6
Textile mill products	4.0	4.5
Apparel and other textile products	2.1	2.4
Lumber and wood products	2.4	3.0
Furniture and fixtures	1.5	1.8
Paper and allied products	2.0	2.7
Printing and publishing	0.9	1.2
Chemicals and allied products	3.0	4.0
Petroleum and coal products	0.8	3.2
Rubber and miscellaneous plastic products	1.8	2.2
Leather and leather products	1.0	1.5
Stone, clay, and glass products	1.4	2.0
Primary metal industries	0.2	1.0
Fabricated metal products	1.4	1.8
Machinery, except electrical	2.8	3.5
Electric and electronic equipment	3.6	4.3
Transportation equipment	1.9	2.5
Instruments and related products	3.0	3.5
Miscellaneous manufacturing	2.5	3.1

Source: Adapted from John W. Kendrick, "Policy Implications of the Slowdown in U.S. Productivity Growth," paper presented at the North Carolina Policy Conference on Productivity Growth and the Competitiveness of the American Economy, Chapel Hill, February 19, 1987, p. 21.

means it helps them in translating economic forecasts into whatever productivity growth experiences are expected to follow within their organization. Second, the factors that follow are microeconomic in nature may be viewed as control variables for managers to use when formulating growth-related strategies for their firms.

Cyclical Shocks: It has been suggested that the productivity slow-downs described earlier are no more than the result of a cyclical shock on the economy. The corresponding experiences in industries are, according to this argument, the manifestation of these shocks. Although the empirical evidence on this point is mixed, we believe that secular trends are the more dominant cause of productivity growth variation. In other words, we believe that the slowdowns were real and need to be understood.

Capital Investments: Changes in the growth of capital are indeed an important factor related to measured productivity growth at both the aggregate level and the level of the firm. Our economy, and many firms within the manufacturing sector of the economy, experienced a slowdown in investments in productive capital. In the U.S. economy, growth in capital per worker decreased by more than one-half between the 1960–1973 period and the 1973–1981 period, 2.1 percent per year to 1.0 percent per year. Relatedly, there is abundant anecdotal evidence that corporate capital investment strategies also changed in the late 1960s and early 1970s in response to other economic trends.

Inflation and Energy Prices: There are sound economic reasons to expect that inflationary tendencies will have a dampening impact on productivity growth, and inflation was very high during the periods under discussion. First, during periods of unanticipated or prolonged inflation, there is less certainly about the information contained in price signals, compared to periods when prices are stable. Because managerial decisions are made in an uncertain climate, there may be efficiency losses as planning horizons shorten. Moreover, forecasting and decision making in compressed time frames may be misguided. For example, as the price of inputs rises during inflationary periods, it becomes increasingly difficult to determine what portion of the increase is general and inflation-induced and what portion reflects changes in *relative* factor costs. Second, managerial talent may be diverted toward short-run decision making as a result of the increased factor-price uncertainty. The ramifications may show up in an inability to estimate correctly hurdle rates for investments and in an altered attitude on the part of managers toward risk taking. Third, in addition to affecting the choice of an optimal input mix, inflationary tendencies can directly affect capital investments. Depreciation of plant and equipment is based on historical costs. As a result, prolonged periods of inflation will lead to a widened gap between historical costs and effective replacement costs. Thus, current profits and taxes on profits are viewed as too high vis-à-vis the level requisite for financing the required investments. One obvious phenomenon linked to the worldwide inflation in the 1970s was the energy crisis of 1973. Some contend that the 1973 crisis was the primary influence bringing about the post-1973 productivity slowdown. This is because the energy shock represented a structural change in production relationships, thus decreasing the overall demand for capital equipment.

Government Regulation: Government regulation may reduce measured productivity growth because the compliance costs in the affected industries and firms are absorbed by diverting resources (financial, technical, and human) from activities that would otherwise increase output. It should be kept in mind that there are benefits from regulation, such as improvements in the value and quality of life, which may not be captured fully in productivity growth measures.

Unionization: One view of unionism predicts that unions will decrease labor productivity by reducing managements' flexibility, introducing inefficient work rules, and limiting compensation based on individual production. In contrast to this view, some economists emphasize a "collective voice–institutional response" view arguing that unionism (a form of collective organization) may increase the level of labor productivity. Unions, in this latter scenario, are said to act as agents for workers by providing a collective bargaining voice. Productivity is enhanced through decreased turnover, seniority systems, and the like. In addition, unionization "shocks" management to reduce inefficiency. The influence of unions on aggregate productivity trends is rather opaque, based on the empirical evidence. The reality is that union coverage in the private sector has been declining since the mid-1950s, and we doubt that unionization will play an important limiting role in future productivity growth trends.

Entrepreneurship: Did the productivity growth slowdown stem from a lack of perception or ability by leaders to exercise entrepreneurial talents? This argument has been advocated on many occasions in the popular press. Obviously, no single "empirical" test will answer this question, but there may be some truth to the notion that the uncertain economic climate in the late 1960s and early 1970s did, so to speak, change the rules of the game—management was less receptive to risk taking than they had been in the past. Albeit an important issue, it remains fuzzy.

R&D Spending: R&D spending exhibited two interesting trends during these slowdowns. At the aggregate level, it decreased as a percentage of Gross National Product; at the microeconomic level, it not only decreased as a percentage of corporate sales (and of corporate profits), but also there was a noticeable trend away from long-term basic research toward short- term product modification (the former category being thought of as that type of activity more in line with truly innovative activities). Writers were quick to notice these trends, and policy makers were equally quick to initiate policies to provide incentives to corporations to increase their R&D activity—assuming that this correlation between trends is synonymous with a causal relationship. Certain of these policy initiatives were discussed in chapter 3.

Influence of Cooperative Research on Productivity Growth

To estimate empirically the influence of cooperative research activity on the productivity growth of the sixty-two cooperative research-active firms in our subsample, we begin with the production function model of total factor productivity discussed earlier. This model has been used extensively by other researchers who have investigated the influence of changes in R&D spending on the productivity growth slowdown discussed in the previous section, as well as by ourselves.

If, in reference to equation (6.1), the inputs are capital, K, labor, L, and technical knowledge, T, then equation (6.1) can be rewritten as

$$Q = A(t)f(K,L,T) \qquad (6.3)$$

This model parallels the conceptual model developed in Chapter 2 and summarized in figure 2–4. Assuming that the relationship in equation (6.3) is of a Cobb-Douglas form and giving a specification to the time-related shift factor, $A(t)$, then

$$Q = Ae^{\lambda t}K^{\alpha}L^{(1-\alpha)}T^{\beta} \qquad (6.4)$$

where λ is a disembodied growth rate parameter, and α and β are output elasticities. Constant returns to scale are assumed only with respect to K and L, as seen in the elasticities. Taking logarithms and differentiating equation (6.4)

$$\dot{Q}/Q = \lambda + \alpha(\dot{K}/K) + (1-\alpha)(\dot{L}/L) + \beta(\dot{T}/T) \qquad (6.5)$$

where the dot notation (·) refers to a time derivative. Total factor productivity growth is thus defined as

$$\dot{A}/A = \dot{Q}/Q - \alpha(\dot{K}/K) - (1-\alpha)(\dot{L}/L) \qquad (6.6)$$

or using the other terms in equation (6.5):

$$\dot{A}/A = \lambda + \beta(\dot{T}/T) \tag{6.7}$$

The parameter β in equation (6.7) is, by definition, the output elasticity of T, written from equation (6.4) as

$$\beta = (\partial Q/\partial T)/T/Q) \tag{6.8}$$

If we substitute for β from the right-hand portion of equation (6.8) into equation (6.7), and rearrange terms, we have

$$\dot{A}/A = \lambda + \rho(\dot{T}/Q) \tag{6.9}$$

where $\rho = (\partial Q/\partial T)$ is the marginal product of technical capital and $\dot{T}$ is the firm's net private investment into the stock of T.

For empirical purposes, using both aggregate and firm-specific data, researchers have assumed that the stock of technical capital is R&D-based and that it does not depreciate or does so very slowly. With this assumption, $\dot{T}$ in the previous equation is usually approximated by the flow of self-financed R&D expenditures in a given time period; that is, by annual R&D investments. When this is done and a stochastic version of equation (6.9) is estimated, the value of the regression coefficient, $\hat{\rho}$, is interpreted as a measure of the rate of return to investments in R&D.

The empirical evidence is overwhelming that R&D spending is a significant correlate with total factor productivity growth, as measured earlier.[3] This conclusion holds for R&D spending as a whole and even more so when R&D spending is disaggregated by its character of use. For example, if R&D is disaggregated into a basic research, applied research, and development trichotomy, the measured returns to basic research would be significantly greater than for the other components. The same is true for process-related R&D as compared to product-related R&D and for long-term R&D as compared to short-term R&D. Such empirical evidence is in concert with the proposition that one factor associated with slowdowns in productivity growth was the then pervasive managerial attitude toward diverting investments into short-term, quick-payoff, product-related activities.

Our empirical analysis is based on alternative versions of equation (6.9). First, the following equation was estimated using the entire survey sample of ninety-two R&D-active firms:

$$\dot{A}/A = \lambda + \rho(R\&D/Q) + \epsilon \tag{6.10}$$

$\dot{A}/A$ is measured for each firm using data on output, capital, and labor for the time period 1982–1986.[4] In this equation, the R&D variable represents the total company-financed R&D expenditures of the firm for 1984, as gathered from our survey. The corresponding regression coefficient approximates the rate of return to R&D, on average, for this sample of firms. As reported in table 6–4, it is 19.3 percent. This estimated value is quite similar to others' estimates for a cross section of manufacturing firms.

Our second estimation divides each firm's company-financed R&D into two broad categories: internal R&D and cooperative R&D. The sum of these two 1984 figures equals total internal R&D, by firm, as used in the first estimation. As shown in table 6–4, for the entire sample of ninety-two firms, the estimated rate of return to internal R&D is 21.7 percent compared to 1.2 percent to cooperative R&D. Note that this latter estimated return is not significantly different from zero, implying that interfirm differences in total factor productivity growth are unrelated to interfirm differences in cooperative research spending. Of course, in this regression, thirty of the ninety-two values on the cooperative R&D variable equal zero since these firms are not active in such activity. Using the subsample of sixty-two firms, the same regression equation was estimated and, as shown in table 6–4, the story remains virtually unchanged. In essence, investments in cooperative R&D do not have a *direct* influence on firms' rates of productivity growth.

These findings should not be that surprising for two reasons. One, our description of the character of cooperative research in Chapter 2 is such

Table 6–4
Estimates of the Returns to Alternative Categories of R&D Spending

Category		Rate of Return Estimate
Total R&D (n = 92)		19.3%*
Internal R&D	n = 92	21.7%**
Cooperative R&D		1.2%
Internal R&D	n = 62	22.1%**
Cooperative R&D		2.4%
Internal R&D in cooperating firms	n = 92	31.7%**
Internal R&D in noncooperating firms		12.9%*

*Significant at the .05 level.
**Significant at the .01 level.

that we do not expect it *directly* to affect productivity growth. Most cooperative research endeavors are geared toward basic or generic activities. With reference to the model of technology development in table 2–4, such investments leverage the efficiency with which a firms used its technical inputs rather than affecting directly the firm's economic performance. And two, the survey data on the quantifiable output from cooperative research investments presented in tables 6–1 and 6–2 suggest that cooperation in research does not, in general, lead to the kinds of output traditionally associated with R&D, even given a lag time, or associated with activities that directly relate to productivity growth.

Accordingly, we estimated a final version of equation (6.10). In that equation all ninety-two firms were used and the R&D variable was interacted with a binary term equaling one for those sixty-two firms that are active in cooperative research, and zero for the thirty that are not. In other words, our model was structured to test for differences in the rate of return to R&D between cooperating and noncooperating firms.

As shown in table 6–4, both rate of return coefficients are significant. In fact, the estimated results are quite dramatic. The rate of return to R&D among cooperative research–active firms is nearly 150 percent greater than among noncooperating firms: 31.7 percent compared to 12.9 percent, respectively. In other words, cooperation does indeed appear to have an *indirect* effect on firms' R&D activities. Cooperation represents an investment in technical knowledge that manifests itself in a more efficient overall R&D program. Presumably this efficiency includes project selection as well as performance, but our data are not able to feather that distinction.

Concluding Statement

It is somewhat disconcerting to conclude a chapter with anything less than a forceful statement of fact, but in this case some words of caution are definitely in order. Managers should not jump to the conclusion that their internal R&D program will double its efficiency once a cooperative research program is in place. Our analysis is descriptive and not prescriptive. The data that we have analyzed suggest quite clearly that, on average, firms cooperating in research enjoy greater R&D efficiencies than those that do not. It may very well be the case that firms that do not cooperate refrain from the activity because they realize that the marginal benefits from it are small. If this is the case, then a management prescription is not "do cooperative research." Instead, the message to R&D vice-presidents engaged in cooperative research ventures is not to look to a direct return from such activities but rather to evaluate the cooperative research investments in light of their indirect effect on the overall R&D program.

7
Case Studies of Cooperative Research Activity

The previous six chapters have provided an overview of several important characteristics associated with cooperative research activity among U.S. manufacturing firms. We attempted in this overview to illustrate various aspects of the economic environment within which cooperation takes place—the policy constraints surrounding such activities and the factors that influence investment into cooperative research activities. The focus of the empirical analyses in these previous chapters was descriptive of cooperative research activity in general, relying on interindustry and interfirm comparisons. We shift gears in this chapter. Here, we report several case studies. Based on field interviews with a number of firms within our subsample of sixty-two cooperative research–active firms, we have summarized some of our observations.

We believe that these cases illustrate well the variety of cooperative research–related issues facing industry today. Our intent in presenting this information is to offer to managers some insights about cooperation that may be useful to them in their ongoing research endeavors and to provide some guideposts for those managers who are about to embark into cooperative research activities. The names of the individuals interviewed, their companies, and their research partners are confidential. However, the facts related to the cases described here are accurate and represented candidly.

Motivating the R&D Scientist

Company A is a small- to medium-sized firm in the fabricated metals product industry, SIC 34. It has been active in informal cooperative R&D programs since the early 1980s. The purpose of its cooperative efforts is to supplement its in-house research capabilities.

In this firm, management has long realized that long-run financial success depends upon its ability to compete against larger domestic firms. At this point in time, foreign competition is not relevant. During previous decades, Company A has met this competitive challenge by being innovative in its introduction of new and improved products, based in large part on the skills of its R&D scientists and its able marketing division. However, given the increasing costs associated with R&D as well as lackluster sales during the mid-1980s, Company A has turned to cooperation as a way of sharing research costs.

Based on discussions with research managers at Company A, we classify this firm as an innovator that uses cooperation as a leapfrog competitive strategy. The R&D vice-president remarked to us that as long as his company can introduce new products ahead of their more imitation-oriented rivals, they will remain profitable (owing to the twelve- to fifteen-month imitative lag period). He noted that "if we didn't operate this way, we would be broke within a year."

This company faced an interesting problem in motivating its R&D scientists, who were active in the cooperative ventures that generally took place at the partners' laboratories. Upon inspection, it was apparent to us, and to the company's management, that their organizational structure was generating the motivational problem.

The firm has what it calls an Outstanding Researchers Award. This award is made twice a year to an outstanding R&D scientist. Although the selection process and criteria for the award were never made explicit to us or to the scientists themselves, it was our impression from discussions with the R&D scientists that selection for this award (which had a significant monetary component) was generally given only to those who successfully championed a new product idea. Subsequent interviews with R&D mangers did not dispel this view.

Given the firm's structure for conducting cooperative research, members of the cooperative team never had an opportunity to initiate innovative ideas or to champion projects. Company A had a predetermined group of R&D scientists that took part in all of the cooperative endeavors. This group traveled a great deal to other laboratories and was always active in facilitating the prearranged research agenda. The focus of the cooperative research endeavors was determined, in general, by Company A's R&D management staff, led by the R&D vice president. Basically, these scientists were functionally disqualified from ever receiving the award, and they did not like that.

We discussed the issue of motivation with upper management and offered our perception of why the motivational problem exists and what could be done to alleviate it. Management expressed surprise that there was a problem in the first place. Their position was that the team of R&D scientists selected to take part in the cooperative research projects was composed of the very best and brightest scientists within the organization. They were under the impression that such an elite group would find reward enough in being chosen to undertake this strategically important research and needed no other motivational incentives. Management was apparently wrong in this case.

Using Cooperative Research to Diversify

Company B is a world leader in the production of a particular component used in advanced electronic equipment. For years it has enjoyed a dominant position within its single line of business in the electric and electronics equipment industry, SIC 36. However, in the early 1980s, it became evident to upper management that diversification was needed for survival in response to the realistic expectation that its product line would become technologically obsolete by the turn of the century.

We were fortunate to visit this company just after it had one full year of experience with its long-range plan for diversification. This plan centered around several strategically chosen cooperative research alliances. Basically, the company was committed to becoming technologically diversified in anticipation of later becoming product-line diversified. R&D managers explained that "the boys upstairs began this business with a sound technological idea and will agree to expand into new markets only if the needed technological base is in place—not before." Specifically,

- The company joined several research consortia in an effort to learn more about burgeoning technologies. They anticipated this knowledge would put the firm in a better position to utilize effectively its in-house research skills. (This reinforces our belief, and empirical evidence, that cooperative research leverages in-house R&D.)

- The company had identified, and was in the process of acquiring, several small firms that produced a variety of components used by the major electronics producers in this country. The purpose of the acquisition was to establish quickly a diversified technology base within the organization.

- The company established research relationships with several major universities active in its particular field of electronics. These relationships were expected to yield benefits to the firm in years to come, after it identified an area of product interest.

In contrast to the experiences of Company A, Company B experienced no problems from cooperation, to date. We mention this case here only to illustrate an interesting situation in which cooperation was used as a strategic device for positioning a firm to diversity effectively in future years.

Gaining a Market Advantage through Process Technology

Company C operates in only one line of business in the food and kindred products industry, SIC 20. Company C is unrivaled domestically, but it faces increasing import competition from two international producers of its final consumer product. It is unfortunate for Company C that these two international companies are perceived by consumers to produce a higher quality product. Rather than compete with these international rivals in terms of quality, Company C decided to compete in terms of price, offering potential consumers a larger quantity of their product at the same price. This cost reduction strategy is being achieved through cooperative research program with suppliers of the relevant process technologies.

Company C works with its suppliers during the research design stages of production. By doing so, it believes a more advanced technology can be produced that will confer a cost advantage to the company when implemented. This appears to be the case. According to the vice-president for research, cooperation with suppliers during the design stages is proving to be very effective in producing more efficient process technology. But, there also appears to be a cost to achieving this savings.

Management perceives, and let us note that the word *perception* was emphasized strongly in our discussions, that the company's in-house R&D department resents the fact that "the fortunes of the company no longer rest with their product-related innovativeness." At the time of writing this scenario, no solutions to this potential problem have been initiated from the top.

Cooperation in Basic Research

The experience of Company D exemplifies the benefits that can result when a firm engages in cooperative research relationships with other firms within the same industry. The situation of Company D parallels directly the theoretical situation illustrated in the graphic model of cooperative behavior presented in Chapter 6. Company D is a major firm within the petroleum and coal products industry, SIC 29. This firm has a sizeable R&D program. Its R&D program was described to us as "exploratory with focus," doing in-house very little of what we have referred to in this book as *basic research*.

This company relies on cooperative research for the scientific information associated with basic research activities; however, some problems have arisen. In particular, in response to the passage of the National Cooperative Research Act of 1984, the firm began to establish formal research relationships with other firms operating in areas related to petroleum products and refining—a second line of business. These cooperative research ventures were funded at the expense of funding for contracted research to some long-favored universities. In other words, the act provided Company D with an incentive to steer its cooperative basic research activities away from university-based centers toward firm-based partnerships.

We have no information as to the quality of the scientific and technical knowledge previously received from these universities nor have we any knowledge of their new relationships. What is interesting, assuming that the quality of the knowledge generated remains unchanged, is that the personnel department in Company D is noticing increased difficulty in recruiting high-quality graduates from the previously financially favored universities (even in a period when activity in the petroleum-related industries is waning).

Managers in this firm learned from this redirection of resources what academicians have long known; namely, one positive benefit to firms from their industry-university relationships is some degree of favored recruitment among graduates.

Cooperative R&D Is a Second-Rate Venture

Stanley T. Crooke, vice-president and president of pharmaceutical R&D at SmithKline Beckman, notes that excellent scientists want to work only with excellent scientists. His analogy is, "We would never expect a great violinist to be recruited into an orchestra by an incompetent or nonmusical person. Violinists care about their craft and they don't want to play in the midst of others who don't have an equal commitment to their craft. Scientists are the same. They won't play for someone who can't read the music."[1] Our interviews in two firms, Company E and Company F, within the chemicals and allied products industry, SIC 28, underscore these beliefs.

These two medium-sized firms have had a long-standing cooperative relationship with one another. Although not competitors in the same end-product market, both benefit from similar investigations into the generic research issues that underlie their technological bases. (At the time of arranging our initial interview schedules, we did not know that two research partners had been selected for site visits.)

Both of these chemical firms had complaints from their R&D scientists that their cooperative endeavors were second rate. In other words, because neither firm was sending its best scientists to the projects, the participants believed that these projects were less important than the research conducted in-house. And, over time, each firm was developing a tendency to send marginally less competent investigators. What was happening parallels the violin scenario. Participating scientists in cooperative endeavors will, without question in our minds, evaluate the importance of their activity in terms of the quality of the resources invested in the task.

Revisiting the Marketing/R&D Interface Issue

It has long been known that conflicts often arise between the marketing and R&D departments within innovative firms. The reason for this tension is understandable. Marketing often likes to define a market need and then relegate to R&D the task of developing the required product or process. Similarly, R&D has a tendency to want to investigate what is technologically feasible, and then leave it to marketing to create a market for the product or process and thus make it profitable.

We observed this type of dissonance when speaking with the R&D management staff from Company G, which is active in the transportation equipment industry, SIC 37. This relatively small firm, small by that industry's standards, experienced an interesting series of events that led to a dissolution of cooperative research relationships with a long-standing partner.

Apparently what had happened was that the other company's marketing department was identifying market needs and then coming to Company G for assistance in the technological development of the needed products. Quite expectedly, Company G's R&D group began to resent marketing-induced dictates from its partner. As one scientist puts it, "I am sick and tired of hearing about how hard we need to work to make their company's product look good." Seeing no direct payoff, other than in a contracted research vein, to 100 percent effort, efficiency among the R&D scientists began to drop off. When Company G's senior R&D managers became involved in the issue (and this took some time, since much of the cooperative research took place at the partner's laboratories), it became clear to them that relationships were best served by ceasing cooperation rather than mending fences.

We do not know how common it is for cooperative relationships to cease exclusively because of personnel-related problems, but we did hear on numerous occasions that whenever marketing was directly involved in setting cooperative directions problems tended to arise. In fact, we would venture to guess that whenever one partner began to view the enterprise as its own pet project, the health of the relationship soon became in danger.

The Issue of Geographic Proximity

Our final case study is not a case study at all; it is a quantified afterthought. When our field-based investigations were completed, it occurred to us that, based only on the small sample of eighteen firms' R&D vice-presidents who were interviewed, there were considerable interfirm differences in where the cooperating partners were located. Of course, geographic location is not a variable under the control of any one firm, either when deciding to cooperate or deciding with whom to cooperate. But, much in the economics literature suggests that efficiency is enhanced with increased monitoring, and closer geographic proximity often allows for greater monitoring.

We again surveyed these eighteen previously interviewed firms to determine the relative success of each of the cooperative endeavors that they described to us and to note the geographic location of the cooperating partners. Using a Likert scale, the R&D vice-president ranked, the relative ease with which each cooperative research project was conducted and completed (1 = very difficult to 5 = very satisfactory). We then correlated these responses with the geographic proximity of the partners, by project. In fifteen of the eighteen cases, we could conclude that when cooperative research partners were in a close proximity, the ease with which the projects were conducted and completed improved. In the other three firms, no conclusion could be made.

Concluding Statement

A number of management issues have been illustrated in the situations described in this chapter. Several lessons can be learned from these case descriptions.

- R&D scientists, like everyone else, respond to incentives. Like everyone else, too, they want to understand their role in the overall agenda of the company and they want to feel important.
- The value of firms' cooperative research endeavors will be perceived by the participants in direct relationship to the quality of the resources devoted to the endeavors.
- Cooperation is a two-way street. All partners must be willing to devote high-quality resources and must be capable of partaking of the successes. When either the cost or the reward system is skewed, problems can easily arise.
- Cooperative partners obviously should not be selected at random. They should also not be selected solely on the basis of their technological skills. Issues to consider in such research marriages include the intangible characteristics of the involved parties; geographic location, but to a lesser extent; and the organizational structure of the partners' firms, including especially the relationship of R&D to marketing.

8
Summary Statement

Wwilliam C. Norris, Control Data Corporation's chief executive
officer, is by no means a newcomer to the cooperative research
arena. We drew on his thoughts in Chapter 2, when we set the
stage for discussing the nature of cooperative research; We draw again on
his insights for our summary statement. Our theme is simple, cooperative
research is an important technology-based strategy for firms to use to better
compete in world markets. With world competition increasing, "[t]he stage
is set for industry initiatives to expand R&D cooperation rapidly. Only
through joint endeavors of companies can the U.S. meet the challenge of its
world leadership in technology, enhance free-market competition, and expand the job opportunities of its citizens and consumer choices."[1] We
embrace Norris's thoughts completely.

Our analysis in the earlier chapters suggests that corporations are indeed responding to foreign competition by allocating an increasing proportion of their R&D budget to cooperative endeavors. This is an encouraging
sign since, as we also show, well-defined innovation-related outputs are
associated with cooperative research, and there are quantifiable productivity growth benefits.

Cooperative research arrangements are growing, not only among industrial firms but also between industry and university, industry and government, and university and government. This trend is present within most
industrial nations. As pervasive as cooperative research relationships appear, we are not yet at the point to offer prescriptions as to how best to
structure these relationships, how best to provide an environment condu-
cive to their continued development, or how best to monitor their success.
Although this book represents a first step in that direction, more needs to
be known. We are only at the point of seeing its birth; as time passes we
must learn more about these organizational-institutional arrangements so
that we can parent knowledgeably.

Notes

Chapter 1. Introduction

1. Albert N. Link and Gregory Tassey, *Strategies for Technology-based Competition: Meeting the New Global Challenge* (Lexington, Mass.: Lexington Books, 1987), chapters 1 and 6.

2. Quoted in Gene Bylinsky, "The New Look at America's Top Lab," *Fortune*, February 1, 1988, p. 61.

3. Tax incentives for R&D have long been part of the U.S. tax code. For several decades firms have been expensing R&D expenditures. This practice was codified in 1954 with the adoption of Section 174 of the Internal Revenue Code.

4. Cooperation in research is not a new phenomenon. Since the turn of the century, firms have been investing in the research efforts of their trade associations. Generally, these endeavors were limited in scope and were not intended to confer a competitive advantage on any firm. Rather, these endeavors were directed toward basic research and to health, safety, and regulatory issues.

5. Quoted in Dan Dimancescu and James Botkin, *The New Alliance: America's R&D Consortia* (Cambridge, Mass: Ballinger, 1986), p. ix.

6. Jonathan B. Levine and John A. Byrne, "Corporate Odd Couples," *Business Week*, July 21, 1986, p. 100.

7. Nils Wilhjelm, Opening Address presented at the European Industrial Research Management Association conference on Cooperation in R&D, Copenhagen, Denmark, June 3–5, 1987.

8. "On Exporting U.S. Technology," *High Technology Business*, November 1987, p. 49.

9. Albert N. Link and Gregory Tassey, *Strategies for Technology-based Competition: Meeting the New Global Challenge*, chapter 4.

Chapter 2. The Nature of Cooperative Research

1. Adam Smith, *The Wealth of Nations*, edited by Edwin Cannan (New York: Modern Library Inc., 1937 [1776]), p. 128.

2. Gene M. Grossman and Carl Shapiro, "Research Joint Ventures: An Antitrust Analysis," *Journal of Law, Economics, and Organization*, Fall 1986, pp. 315–37.

3. Kathryn Rudie Harrigan, *Strategies for Joint Ventures* (Lexington, Mass: Lexington Books, 1985), chapter 10.

4. Gene M. Grossman and Carl Shapiro, "Research Joint Ventures: An Antitrust Analysis," pp. 332–35.

5. This section draws from Albert N. Link and Gregory Tassey, *Strategies for Technology-based Competition: Meeting the New Global Challenge* (Lexington, Mass: Lexington Books, 1987), chapter 2.

6. David Ford and Chris Ryan, "Taking Technology to Market," *Harvard Business Review*, March-April 1981, pp. 117–26.

7. Robert F. Hebert and Albert N. Link, *The Entrepreneur: Mainstream Views and Radical Critiques*, second edition (New York: Praeger, 1988).

8. James M. Utterback and William J. Abernathy, "A Dynamic Model of Process and Product Innovation," *Omega: The International Journal of Management Science*, December 1975, pp. 639–56.

9. Barry Bozeman and Albert N. Link, *Investments in Technology: Corporate Strategies and Public Policy Alternatives* (New York: Praeger, 1983), pp. 12–16.

10. Quoted in Dwight B. Davis, "R&D Consortia," *High Technology*, October 1985, p. 42.

11. Quoted in Dwight B. Davis, Ibid.

12. William C. Norris, "How to Expand R&D Cooperation," *Business Week*, April 11, 1983, p. 21.

Chapter 3. Public Policy and Cooperative Research

1. Albert N. Link and Gregory Tassey, *Strategies for Technology-based Competition: Meeting the New Global Challenge* (Lexington, Mass.: Lexington Books, 1987), chapter 4.

2. Albert N. Link, *Technological Change and Productivity Growth* (London: Harwood Academic Publishers, 1987).

3. Albert N. Link and Gregory Tassey, *Strategies for Technology-based Competition: Meeting the New Global Challenge*, pp. 75–81.

4. Quoted in Alan Murray, "Tax Reform May Hurt Before It Helps," *Wall Street Journal*, August 4, 1986, p. 22.

5. Quoted in *Antitrust Guide Concerning Research Joint Ventures* (Washington, D.C.: U.S. Department of Justice, 1980), p. i.

6. *Antitrust Guide Concerning Research Joint Ventures*, Ibid., pp. 1–3.

7. Gene M. Grossman and Carl Shapiro, "Research Joint Ventures: An Antitrust Analysis," *Journal of Law, Economics, and Organization*, Fall 1986, pp. 316–17.

8. Important discussions on issues related to the National Cooperative Research Act are in William F. Baxter, "Antitrust Law and Technological Innovation," *Issues in Science and Technology*, Winter 1985, pp. 80–91; Daniel C. Schwartz and J. Michael Cooper, "Antitrust Policy and Technological Innovation: A Response," *Issues in Science and Technology*, Spring 1985, pp. 128–35; and in John T. Scott, "Historical and Economic Perspectives on the National Cooperative Research Act," in *Cooperative Research: A New Strategy for Competition*, A.N. Link and G. Tassey, eds. (Norwell, Mass.: Kluwer Academic Publishers, forthcoming 1989).

9. Kathryn L. Combs, "A Summary of Research Joint Ventures Filed with the Justice Department," unpublished mimeograph, August, 1986.

10. Four of these categories parallel those in Herbert I. Fusfeld and Carmela S. Haklisch, "Cooperative R&D for Competitors," *Harvard Business Review*, November-December 1985, pp. 60–76.

11. William Norris reports that Control Data Corporation committed $14 million to MCC and received access in its first three years to R&D results costing about $119 million. See William C. Norris, "Cooperative R&D: A Regional Strategy," *Issues in Science and Technology*, Winter 1985, p. 94.

12. Ibid.

Chapter 4. Factors Affecting Cooperative Research Activities

1. This section is an extension of earlier work by Albert N. Link and Laura L. Bauer, "An Economic Analysis of Cooperative Research," *Technovation*, October 1987, pp. 247–60.

2. An early investigation of interindustry differences in research joint ventures is in Sanford Berg, Jerome Duncan, and Philip Friedman, *Joint Venture Strategies and Corporate Innovation* (Cambridge, Mass.: Oelgeschlager, Gunn & Hain, 1982), chapter 5.

3. This argument follows from Morton I. Kamien and Nancy L. Schwartz, "Self-financing of an R&D Project," *American Economic Review*, June 1978, pp. 252–61.

4. Ira Horowitz, "Estimating Changes in the Research Budget," *Journal of Industrial Engineering*, March 1961, pp. 114–18.

5. This literature is reviewed in great detail in William L. Baldwin and John T. Scott, *Market Structure and Technological Change* (London: Harwood Academic Publishers, 1987).

6. Four-digit categories outside of the manufacturing sector were ignored. Concentration data correspond to 1982, as reported by the Bureau of Census. The results presented below are invariant to the use of adjusted 1977 industry concentration ratios, as developed by Weiss and Pasoce. See, Leonard W. Weiss and George A. Pascoe, Jr., *Adjusted Concentration Ratios in Manufacturing, 1972 and 1977* (Washington, D.C.: Federal Trade Commission, 1986).

7. Referring to the distribution of sample firms in table 4–2, firms in industries SIC 22, 27, 30, and 31 were included in the intercept term.

8. This interpretation draws directly from discussions with John McDonald and Terry Seaks. See, John F. McDonald and Robert A. Moffitt, "The Uses of Tobit Analysis," *Review of Economics and Statistics*, May 1980, pp. 318–20.

9. This appendix is based, in part, on findings presented in Albert N. Link and Robert W. Zmud, "R&D Patterns in the Video Display Terminal Industry," *Journal of Product Innovation Management*, September 1984, pp. 106–15. See also the references noted therein.

Chapter 5. Cooperative Research as a Competitive Strategy

1. Roland W. Schmitt, "Company Policies for Technical Cooperation," paper presented at the European Industrial Research Management Association conference on Cooperation in R&D, Copenhagen, Denmark, June 3–5, 1987, p. 1.

2. This section draws from Albert N. Link and Gregory Tassey, *Strategies for Technology-based Competition: Meeting the New Global Challenge* (Lexington, Mass.: Lexington Books, 1987), chapter 2.

3. For a similar study of European firms see, P. Mariti and R.H. Smiley, "Cooperative Agreements and the Organization of Industry," *Journal of Industrial Economics*, June 1983, pp. 437–51.

4. These binary variables equal 1 for the following seven two-digit industries and zero otherwise: SIC 20, SIC 28, SIC 29, SIC 35, SIC 36, SIC 37, and SIC 38.

5. The empirical analysis that follows was a precursor to our development of the conceptual arguments presented in the first part of chapter 5 and to the formulation of the survey instrument used in gathering data on firms' cooperative research strategies. The description that follows draws from Albert N. Link and John L. Neufeld, "Innovation versus Imitation: Investigating Alternative R&D Strategies," *Applied Economics*, December 1986, pp. 1359–63.

Chapter 6. Cooperative Research and the Production of Knowledge

1. This section draws from Barry Bozeman, Albert N. Link, and Asghar Zardkoohi, "An Economic Analysis of R&D Joint Ventures," *Managerial and Decision Economics*, August 1986, pp. 263–66.

2. For a more detailed discussion of this topic see Albert N. Link, *Technological Change and Productivity Growth* (London: Harwood Academic Publishers, 1987), and the references therein.

3. Ibid., pp. 53–57.

4. The formulation of such a residual measure of total factor productivity is well known. The primary data come from Compustat. A complete description of the methodology for these calculations is in Barry Bozeman and Albert N. Link, *Investments in Technology: Corporate Strategies and Public Policy Alternatives* (New York: Praeger, 1983), pp. 77–78.

Chapter 7. Case Studies of Cooperative Research Activity

1. Quoted in Michael F. Wolff, "Attracting First-Class Scientists," *Research Management*, November-December, 1987, p. 9.

Chapter 8. Summary Statement

1. William C. Norris, "How to Expand R&D Cooperation," *Business Week*, April 11, 1983, p. 21.

References

Baldwin, William L., and John T. Scott. 1987. *Market Structure and Technological Change*. London: Harwood Academic Publishers.

Baxter, William F. 1985. "Antitrust Law and Technological Innovation." *Issues in Science and Technology* (Winter): 80–91.

Berg, Sanford, Jerome Duncan, and Philip Friedman. 1982. *Joint Venture Strategies and Corporate Innovation*. Cambridge, Mass.: Oelgeschlager, Gunn & Hain.

Bozeman, Barry, and Albert N. Link. 1983. *Investments in Technology: Corporate Strategies and Public Policy Alternatives*. New York: Praeger.

Bozeman, Barry, Albert N. Link, and Asghar Zardkoohi. 1986. "An Economic Analysis of R&D Joint Ventures." *Managerial and Decision Economics* (August): 263–66.

Bylinsky, Gene. 1988. "The New Look at America's Top Lab." *Fortune* (February 1), p. 61.

Combs, Kathryn L. 1986. "A Summary of Research Joint Ventures Filed with the Justice Department." Unpublished mimeograph.

Davis, Dwight B. 1985. "R&D Consortia," *High Technology* (October): 42–47.

Dimancescu, Dan, and James Botkin. 1986. *The New Alliance: America's R&D Consortia*. Cambridge, Mass.: Ballinger.

Ford, David, and Chris Ryan. 1981. "Taking Technology to Market." *Harvard Business Review* (March–April): 117–26.

Fusfeld, Herbert I., and Carmela S. Haklisch. 1985. "Cooperative R&D for Competitors." *Harvard Business Review* (November–December): 60–76.

Grossman, Gene M., and Carl Shapiro. 1986. "Research Joint Ventures: An Antitrust Analysis." *Journal of Law, Economics, and Organization* (Fall): 315–37.

Harrigan, Kathryn Rudie. 1985. *Strategies for Joint Ventures*. Lexington, Mass.: Lexington Books.

Hébert, Robert F., and Albert N. Link. 1988. *The Entrepreneur: Mainstream Views and Radical Critiques*, 2d ed. New York: Praeger.

Horowitz, Ira. 1961. "Estimating Changes in the Research Budget." *Journal of Industrial Engineering* (March): 114–18.

Kamien, Morton I., and Nancy L. Schwartz. 1978. "Self-financing of an R&D Project." *American Economic Review* (June): 252–61.

Levine, Jonathan B., and John A. Bryne. 1986. "Corporate Odd Couples." *Business Week* (July 21), p. 100.

Link, Albert N. 1987. *Technological Change and Productivity Growth*. London: Harwood Academic Publishers.

Link, Albert N., and Laura L. Bauer. 1987. "An Economic Analysis of Cooperative Research." *Technovation* (October): 247–60.

Link, Albert N., and John L. Neufeld. 1986. "Innovation versus Imitation: Investigating Alternative R&D Strategies." *Applied Economics* (December): 1359–63.

Link, Albert N., and Gregory Tassey. 1987. *Strategies for Technology-Based Competition: Meeting the New Global Challenge*. Lexington, Mass.: Lexington Books.

Link, Albert N., and Robert W. Zmud. 1984. "R&D Patterns in the Video Display Terminal Industry." *Journal of Product Innovation Management* (September): 106–15.

McDonald, John F., and Robert A. Moffitt. 1980. "The Uses of Tobit Analysis." *Review of Economics and Statistics* (May): 318–20.

Martini, P., and R. H. Smiley. 1983. "Co-operative Research Agreements and the Organization of Industry." *Journal of Industrial Economics* (June): 437–51.

Murray, Alan. 1986. "Tax Reform May Hurt before It Helps." *Wall Street Journal* (August 4), p. 22.

Norris, William C. 1985. "Cooperative R&D: A Regional Strategy." *Issues in Science and Technology* (Winter): 92–102.

Norris, William C. 1983. "How to Expand R&D Cooperation." *Business Week* (April 11), p. 21.

Schmitt, Roland W. 1987. "Company Policies for Technical Cooperation," paper presented at the European Industrial Research Management Association conference on Cooperation in R&D, Copenhagen, Denmark, June 3–5.

Schwartz, Daniel C., and J. Michael Cooper. 1985. "Antitrust Policy and Technological Innovation: A Response." *Issues in Science and Technology* (Spring): 128–35.

Scott, John T. Forthcoming 1989. "Historical and Economic Perspectives on the National Cooperative Research Act." In *Cooperative Research: A New Strategy for Competition*, ed. A. N. Link and G. Tassey, Norwell, Mass.: Kluwer Academic Publishers.

Smith, Adam. 1937 [1776]. *The Wealth of Nations*, ed. Edwin Cannan. New York: Modern Library, Inc.

U.S. Department of Justice. 1980. *Antitrust Guide Concerning Research Joint Ventures*. Washington, D.C.: U.S. Department of Justice.

Utterback, James M., and William J. Abernathy. 1975. "A Dynamic Model of Process and Product Innovation." *Omega: The International Journal of Management Science* (December): 639–56.

Weiss, Leonard W., and George A. Pascoe, Jr. 1986. *Adjusted Concentration Ratios in Manfacturing, 1972 and 1977*. Washington, D.C.: Federal Trade Commission. 1986.

Wilhjelm, Nils. 1987. Opening address presented at the European Industrial Research Management Association conference on Cooperation in R&D, Copenhagen, Denmark, June 3–5.

Wolff, Michael F. 1987. "Attracting First-Class Scientists." *Research Management* (November–December): 9.

Index

About the Authors

Albert N. Link is professor of economics and director of the Industrial Technology Program at the University of North Carolina at Greensboro. Since receiving a Ph.D. from Tulane University in 1976, he has written extensively in the areas of productivity, technology change, and innovation policy. In addition to numerous journal articles and technical reports, he is the author or coauthor of nine books including *Strategies for Technology-Based Competition: Meeting the New Global Challenge.*

Laura L. Bauer is a research associate at Quick, Finan & Associates. She completed her M.A. degree in applied economics at the University of North Carolina at Greensboro in 1988. Specializing in R&D economics and science policy, her previous writings have appeared in *Technovation* and other collected volumes.